HEROES OF HISTORY

DANIEL BOONE

Frontiersman

JANET & GEOFF BENGE

Emerald Books

P.O. BOX 635, LYNNWOOD, WA 98046

Emerald Books are distributed through YWAM Publishing. For a full list of titles, including other great biographies, visit our website at www.emerald-books.com.

Library of Congress Cataloging-in-Publication Data

Benge, Janet, 1958–
Daniel Boone : frontiersman / by Janet and Geoff Benge.
p. cm. — (Heroes of history)
Includes bibliographical references.
ISBN 1-932096-09-4
1. Boone, Daniel, 1734–1820—Juvenile literature. 2. Pioneers—Kentucky—Biography—Juvenile literature. 3. Explorers—Kentucky—Biography—Juvenile literature. 4. Frontier and pioneer life—Kentucky—Juvenile literature. 5. Kentucky—Biography—Juvenile literature. 6. Kentucky—Discovery and exploration—Juvenile literature. I. Benge, Geoff, 1954– II. Title.
F454.B66B46 2004
976.9'02'092—dc22 2004001741

Daniel Boone: Frontiersman

Second edition 2009

Published by Emerald Books
P.O. Box 635
Lynnwood, WA 98046

ISBN 978-1-932096-09-5 (paperback)
ISBN 978-1-932096-70-5 (e-book)

Sixth printing 2024

Printed in the United States of America

HEROES OF HISTORY

DANIEL BOONE

Frontiersman

HEROES OF HISTORY

Abraham Lincoln
Alan Shepard
Ben Carson
Benjamin Franklin
Benjamin Rush
Billy Graham
Captain John Smith
Christopher Columbus
Clara Barton
Davy Crockett
Daniel Boone
Douglas MacArthur
Dwight Eisenhower
Elizabeth Fry
Ernest Shackleton
Frederick Douglass
George Washington
George Washington Carver
Harriet Tubman
John Adams
Laura Ingalls Wilder
Louis Zamperini
Meriwether Lewis
Milton Hershey
Orville Wright
Ronald Reagan
Theodore Roosevelt
Thomas Edison
William Bradford
William Penn
William Wilberforce
Winston Churhill

Available in paperback, e-book, and audiobook formats.
Curriculum Guides are available for all of the U.S. biographies.
www.Heroesofhistory.com

(WISC.)
(MICH.)
NEW YORK
(IOWA)
DETROIT
PENNSYLVANIA
EXETER
N.J.
(OHIO)
(ILLINOIS)
(IND.)
CHILLICOTHE
MD.
DEL.
FEMME OSAGE
LIMESTONE
(W. VIRGINIA)
ST LOUIS
BLUE LICKS
VIRGINIA
BOONE'S STATION
BOONESBOROUGH
(MO.)
(KENTUCKY)
CASTLE'S WOOD
Cumberland Gap
N. CAROLINA
YADKIN
(TENNESSEE)
(ARK.)
S. CAROLINA
(MISS.)
GEORGIA
(ALABAMA)
(LA.)
PENSACOLA
(FLORIDA)
ST. AUGUSTINE
N
W
E
S

Contents

Chapter 1

Escape

Sheltowee, Sheltowee. Don't do it!" his adoptive mother yelled in Algonquian. "They will catch you and kill you, Sheltowee, come back to me!"

As Sheltowee tucked his head and urged the horse forward at full gallop, he tried to shut out the Indian woman's wail. He knew he was in the race of his life. He could not let his tumultuous emotions distract him from getting back home to Boonesborough. He had to think of what lay ahead; with one careless move, not only his own life but also the lives of his wife and children and many other settlers would be lost.

For the past several months, since his capture by Shawnee Indians, he had been Sheltowee, or Big Turtle, the adopted son of Chief Blackfish, with his head plucked bare except for a warrior's single lock and wearing painted breechcloth pants. But he was also Daniel, the son of Squire and Sarah Boone. Daniel's father had originally emigrated from England, while his mother was born in America. And right now Daniel's wife and children and the other settlers living in the small community of Boonesborough beside the Kentucky River were in grave peril. Daniel had learned from his captors that in just a few days a large raiding party of Shawnee warriors intended to attack and destroy Boonesborough and either kill its residents or carry them away as prisoners. Daniel could not let that happen. He had to try to sound the alarm, even if it cost him his life.

Thankfully, Daniel had at least a half-hour lead on the Shawnee warriors who would surely pursue him. He knew they were able horsemen and quite capable of overtaking him, and so he rode on like the wind until his horse gave out. He let the animal go in a thicket and continued on foot, using every bit of woodcraft he knew to hide his tracks. He ran through brushwood, jumped over boulders, and waded down creek beds.

When night fell, Daniel dropped from exhaustion. He dared not light a fire, and he had no food, so he lay down on a pile of leaves and quickly fell asleep. When the moon was high, he was awakened by something seizing one of his toes. His heart thumped in terror as he sat up, fully expecting to find himself surrounded by Shawnee warriors. Instead he caught a glimpse of a mischievous fox scampering off into the undergrowth.

Daniel was so tired he went straight back to sleep and did not wake up until sunrise. By then his feet were aching from running in wet moccasins all the previous day. But there was no time to lose, so he put his soggy moccasins back on and continued heading south.

All the next day and the day after that Daniel traveled, urged on by the thought of his family at home in the rough-hewn stockade, under threat of a massive Indian attack. As he ran for his life and the lives of others, Daniel knew he was caught in an adventure far beyond what he had ever been able to imagine as a boy back in Pennsylvania, where he roamed the woods and dreamed of the frontier.

Chapter 2

A Love of the Outdoors

Five-year-old Daniel Boone stared at the barred cabin door. "It ain't fair!" he said to his mother.

"Let's not get into that again, Daniel," she chided. "You'll just have to accept it. There's a lot of smallpox about, and you can't go outside and play with the neighbor children. You might catch the illness from one of them."

Daniel wanted to ask what was so awful about that, but he held his tongue. Everyone knew that smallpox could make people very sick or even kill them, but staying inside the cabin, cooped up with his six brothers and sisters, seemed just about as bad to Daniel as having smallpox.

Daniel's seven-year-old sister, Elizabeth, signaled to him. "I have an idea," she whispered. "Come up to the loft."

Dutifully Daniel followed her up the ladder and plunked himself down on his chaff-filled mattress.

"You know why we ain't allowed to go outside and play with the other children, don't you?" Elizabeth asked.

"'Cause we might catch the pox off one of them," Daniel replied.

"Well," Elizabeth went on, "I've been thinking about this mighty hard, and I reckon if we did catch the pox and then got better, we would be able to play with all the other children who've had it. Don't you think?"

Daniel tried hard to follow her reasoning. "But the pox is bad," he said.

"Not as bad as staying here in the cabin day after day," Elizabeth replied.

Daniel nodded. He and Elizabeth felt the same about being outside. They liked the same activities, such as playing in the woods and making up Indian stories and having peashooting competitions. So their mother's new rules were difficult for both of them, unlike for their oldest sister, Sarah, who spent all day helping her mother around the cabin and seemed to enjoy it.

"How could we catch the pox and get it over with?" Daniel asked.

"We go play with the Clausen children, silly. All of them have it."

"But how will we get out of the cabin without Ma catching us?" Daniel wondered, glancing down at the barred door.

"Do I have to think of everything?" Elizabeth asked with a sigh. "After dark, when everyone's asleep, we open the door and creep out. When we get to the Clausen cabin, we climb the outside ladder to the upstairs loft and knock on the trapdoor. The children are bound to let us in—they're probably just as bored as we are—and then we can catch the pox off them. What do you think?"

What did he think? Escaping from the house in the middle of the night, sneaking into the Clausens' cabin, and catching the pox so he could play with his friends again. It sounded like an adventure! It sounded great!

The rest of the day dragged on. Daniel's mother, Sarah, let him outside for a few minutes to collect kindling for the fire, but he was on strict instructions not to go more than a few paces from the cabin.

A squirrel and then a jackrabbit crossed Daniel's path, and Daniel ached to have his slingshot in his hands. How wonderful it would be to roam the woods again.

That night, when everyone was asleep, Elizabeth and Daniel crept down the ladder. Slowly Daniel lifted the bar on the door and pushed it open. It was a moonlit night, and soon they were off, hand in hand, around their father's blacksmith shop and along the rough track that led into the Pennsylvania forest.

When they reached the Clausens' cabin, everything went as planned. Samuel, the oldest Clausen boy, let Daniel and Elizabeth in, and soon they were all sitting side by side telling scary stories. Daniel made sure his knees touched Samuel's and that he took deep breaths of the smallpox-infected air. After about half an hour everyone got sleepy, and the two Boone children climbed down the ladder and headed for home.

Five days later Daniel was not so sure he had done the right thing. His throat burned, and welts were popping up all over his body. His mother took one look at him and said, "Now, Daniel, I want you to tell me the truth. How did you get the pox when you were forbidden to play with the other children?"

Daniel looked around for Elizabeth, but she was still in the loft. He would have to face this alone. "I...I, we went to see Samuel and the other Clausen children," he stammered.

Sarah Boone took a step back. Her face went white. "Why didn't you tell me?" she cried. "I could have been better prepared. Now we will all come down with the pox!"

Daniel fixed his gaze on the braided rug at his feet. He hadn't thought of that. He and Elizabeth had put the whole family, even three-year-old Mary, at risk. Suddenly he felt very ashamed of his actions.

"Well, get yourself into bed," his mother sighed. "We'll have to get this over and done with now that it's begun. And may God have mercy on us all."

Daniel spent the rest of that week and most of the following week fighting a high temperature. Soon all of his brothers and sisters, including Elizabeth, had come down with smallpox. Daniel feared the worst. Thankfully, however, everyone in the family recovered from the dreadful disease.

When Daniel finally got better, he was allowed to play in the woods again. As he ran along the trail to tell the Clausen children the good news, he promised himself that when he grew up, he would never be confined to a cabin again. His place was in the forest, running free like the wild turkeys and the deer.

In 1744, five years after the smallpox outbreak, the Boone clan had grown to ten children. Each of the older children had a specific job to do. Sarah, the oldest Boone daughter, had married a German immigrant named John Wilcoxen two years before, and much to her disappointment, Elizabeth had had to take over Sarah's indoor chores. Daniel's oldest brother, Israel, worked in his father's blacksmith shop, along with an apprentice named Henry Miller.

Along with the blacksmith shop, the Boone farm had a separate weaving cabin in which six looms were set up. Daniel's father, Squire Boone, had emigrated from England as a teenager with his older brother and sister. The rest of the Boone clan had followed them to America several years later. Once in the New World, Squire Boone had followed in the family business of weaving. The looms produced a rough fabric, made of a combination of wool and linen, called linsey-woolsey. Squire's sons Samuel and Jonathan, the next two brothers, worked the looms along with Mary. Daniel, because of his love for the outdoors, was in charge of gathering berries and bringing home wild game. His father thought he was still too young at ten to have his own gun, but just by throwing a wooden club, Daniel could kill a rabbit at ten yards.

During the summer of 1744 Daniel received the best news of all. His father had become so successful that he was able to buy a twenty-five-acre tract of land in Oley, six miles north of the Boone homestead at Exeter, where he intended to graze cattle. This task required two people, one to watch out for the cows and herd them into the cow pens each evening and another to milk the animals and make butter and cheese from their milk.

Since the land was too far away to drive the cows back and forth each day, it was decided that Daniel and his mother should spend the rest of the summer together on the new land. Daniel could not have been happier, and when he and his father had finished building a rough-hewn log cabin on the site, they drove the milking cows to the new property.

A stream ran across the land, supplying their water, and they had an abundance of dairy products and wild game to eat. In the evenings Daniel's mother cooked over an open fire, often singing early American songs of her youth as she worked. Once a week Sarah Boone would take the butter and cheese she had made back to the homestead to store it in the cellar. Each time, Daniel proudly provided her with some wild game to take along as well. At first Daniel thought he would feel lonely or even a little afraid, staying by himself on the land overnight while his mother was away, but he soon learned to love being alone in the forest. He studied the birds and small animals until he knew every sound they made and the telltale tracks that each left. Daniel was not even scared of the panthers that prowled the area.

The carefree summer was interrupted by sad news. Daniel's grandfather, George Boone III, died unexpectedly. George Boone III had been a pillar in the Quaker community, and he left behind eight children, fifty-two grandchildren, and ten great grandchildren.

Daniel thought sadly of the stories about life among the early colonists that his grandfather used to tell him. One of his favorites was about an encounter between Indians and settlers that occurred at Manatawny in 1728. A group of Shawnee Indians had gotten into a fight with a group of colonists who had refused to give them food. Gunfire followed, and one of the Shawnee was wounded. Manatawny was just ten miles from the Boone farm, and since the Shawnees had fled in their direction, news of the incident threw the small community into a panic. Daniel's grandfather sent a dispatch to the colonial governor asking for help to defend their farms. "We are resolved to defend ourselves to ye last Extremity," he told the governor in the dispatch. Sure enough, a group of Shawnee men did show up, but the colonists were so afraid that they let them eat all they wanted. When the Indians finally fled into the forest, Daniel's grandfather led about twenty men after them. A gun battle erupted when they caught up with the Shawnees, and two of the settlers were wounded.

It wasn't the most adventurous story that Daniel had ever heard, but it was about the most exciting Indian story in Pennsylvania. Daniel knew that other colonies had much more exciting clashes with the Indians, but then the people in those colonies weren't Quakers, trying to live at peace with all men. Other Indian tribes from all over the colonies knew that they could find safety in William Penn's colony, and many of them migrated there. Missionaries now worked among the Indians, and only a short distance from the new property at Oley, Daniel had seen Moravian missionaries baptizing a number of new converts among the Delaware Indians.

After his grandfather's funeral, the rest of the summer went by quickly for Daniel. In the fall, Daniel's father declared that since his son had handled his responsibilities like a man, the man should have his own rifle. Daniel, thrilled with the thought of having his own rifle at last, could not agree more.

Chapter 3

Growing Up

Daniel held his muzzle-loading rifle with both hands. He had watched his older brothers and father shoot so many times that it took him only a few days to adjust to the kickback of the rifle when he pulled the trigger. Within two weeks Daniel had become an accurate shot.

One night, several weeks after Daniel had received the rifle, a number of the boys from the village of Exeter decided it would be fun to go into the woods at night and try their hand at some hunting. Daniel was eager to join them, but he knew that his parents would never give him permission to do so. Daniel's solution was to not ask them. Instead he waited until the family was asleep. He then sneaked out of the house and made his way to the barn, where Henry Miller, the apprentice from the blacksmith shop, who was two years older than Daniel, met him. Together they saddled up Squire Boone's best horse and galloped off into the night. They followed the trail into the woods and soon found the other boys. Daniel tied up the horse, and together all the boys stalked through the forest looking for wild game.

No matter how quiet the boys tried to be, such a large group of boys creeping through the forest seemed to alert the wild animals to their presence. After several hours the young hunters had not seen a single animal to shoot and so decided to give up the hunt. Daniel was disappointed; he had wanted a chance to show off his expert shooting.

Daniel retrieved his father's horse, and he and Henry climbed onto the animal's back. Daniel dug his heels into the horse's sides, and they were off at a full gallop. The wind tousled Daniel's hair as they raced through the pitch blackness. The horse turned into the lane that led to the Boone farm, and Daniel urged the animal on, trying to make it go faster on the homestretch. It was an especially exhilarating ride, Daniel silently admitted, because it was a ride he wasn't even supposed to be on. Then he saw the cow lying right in the middle of the lane. He had no time to stop. All Daniel could do was grab the reins tighter and urge the horse to jump over the cow. As the horse was leaping, the startled cow stumbled to its feet. The two animals collided, sending Daniel and Henry tumbling to the ground with a thud. It took the boys a few moments to recover from the fall, and when they finally got their bearings, the cow had run off. But not the horse. It lay dead on the path, its head tilted at an unnatural angle. Daniel gasped in horror as he realized that the horse had broken its neck in the collision with the cow.

"What are we going to do now?" Henry wailed. "That was your father's best horse."

Daniel panicked. "Let's just leave the horse here. In the morning Father will discover it and think it escaped from the barn and had some unfortunate accident." He reached under the horse's girth. "Here, help me get the saddle and bridle off."

The two boys worked together, and soon the saddle was swung over Daniel's shoulder while Henry carried the bridle. They were nearly home when Daniel suddenly remembered something. "My rifle!" he exclaimed. "It came off my shoulder when I fell, and I was so shocked by the dead horse that I forgot to pick it up. I have to go back and get it."

Daniel dropped the saddle and ran off into the darkness to fetch his prized new possession. After several minutes of scratching around in the dark, Daniel located his rifle half under a bush. He slung it over his shoulder and ran back to where Henry was waiting. The two of them placed the saddle and bridle back in the barn, and Daniel sneaked back into the house.

The following morning Daniel found his father standing in the blacksmith shop talking to Daniel's oldest brother, Israel. Henry was sharpening nails in the corner.

"I don't understand it," Daniel heard his father say. "She was locked in the barn. I don't know how she managed to get out, since the barn door was still closed this morning, and more mysterious still, how did the animal manage to break its neck?" Squire Boone scratched his head as he spoke.

Daniel's stomach lurched. He said nothing and ran out of the shop before his father could notice him. He dared not look in Henry's direction. He just had to get out of there.

Not long afterward, Daniel's overconfident attitude towards rifles again led him and Henry into mischief. This time it involved playing a joke on George Wilcoxen, a cousin of John Wilcoxen, the husband of Daniel's sister Sarah.

George, who was staying at the Boone house, had little practical knowledge of guns. When Daniel and Henry discovered George's loaded rifle in the house, they saw it as an opportunity to have a little fun. They knew that George was going hunting in the morning, and that being nervous about handling guns, George had asked Daniel's father to load it for him. While George slept, Daniel took the loaded rifle, and he and Henry carefully removed the musket ball. Then they poured in a lot more gunpowder, enough gunpowder for five shots, and gently replaced the ball, putting the gun back in its resting place.

The following morning Daniel was awakened by what sounded like a cannon going off. Suddenly he recalled the trick he had played on George and leaped out of bed. He ran outside just in time to see George come into view. Daniel was startled to see that George's face was bloodied and bruised and he had a large gash on his forehead.

"Did you hear that boom?" Daniel asked, trying to sound matter-of-fact.

"It was that darned gun," George began. "When I pulled the trigger, it threw me backward with such force I landed face-first against a stump."

Daniel's father was once again mystified. "How can this be?" he asked George. "I put only a light load in the rifle, nowhere near enough powder to send you recoiling backward with the force you say." Once again he scratched his head, and this time Daniel gave Henry a knowing glance.

The incident, however, did have a sobering effect on Daniel, who now realized that joking around with a rifle was too dangerous. With so much gunpowder, the muzzle of the rifle could very well have exploded in George's face and killed him. Daniel promised himself that he would never again fool around with rifles—his or anyone else's. From now on, he would use his expert gun-handling skills for a better, more useful purpose.

The summer of 1747 saw Daniel and Elizabeth back on the tract of land at Oley. They helped tend the cows and run the dairy because their mother was taking care of the newest Boone baby, a girl named Hannah. This brought the number of Boone children to eleven and made Daniel the middle child. As the family's best marksman, Daniel was again in charge of hunting for the family's food. Throughout the summer, he shot more than enough game to feed his entire family. He even had enough game left over to exchange for gunpowder, lead, and flints to last through the winter.

Daniel and Elizabeth returned home to the Boone farm in the fall, just in time for a wedding. Their oldest brother, Israel, was marrying a Dutch girl. It should have been a joyous occasion, but it turned out to be one that split the family down the middle. The young woman was not a Quaker, and faithful Quakers did not marry "worldlings," people who were not Quakers. As a result, the wedding announcement set off a whirlwind of controversy. And it was not the first time that this had happened in the Boone family. Daniel's oldest sister, Sarah, had also married a worldling five years before. In that instance Daniel's parents had been summoned before a committee of Quakers and told they would have to publicly acknowledge their mistake in allowing their daughter to be courted by a German Lutheran. The committee required both of Daniel's parents to draft a written confession of their wrong and promise never to allow any of their other children to marry someone who wasn't Quaker.

When Israel announced his marriage engagement, the committee was not as forgiving toward the Boone family as it had been in the past. It asked Squire and Sarah Boone for an explanation as to why they had allowed a second child to entertain the idea of what it considered a "disorderly marriage."

This time Squire Boone had had enough. He did not believe that an explanation was necessary, and he refused to write a letter even though Daniel's mother begged him to. As a result the Quaker committee banned him from attending their meetings. His wife, on the other hand, submitted to church discipline and remained a Quaker in good standing.

This turn of events was confusing for thirteen-year-old Daniel. His grandparents had been Quakers, as were his numerous aunts, uncles, and cousins, all of whom had homesteads in the area. He was not sure what to do. Should he continue attending meetings with his mother or side with his father?

While Daniel was still fretting about this, yet another wedding took place in the family. Daniel's second oldest brother, Samuel, married Sarah Day, a devout Quaker. Daniel liked Sarah a great deal; she was kind and smart. In fact, unlike Daniel's mother, she could read and write. The newlyweds moved into a nearby cabin, and Sarah soon made Daniel's education her personal project. A winter school had been held off and on through the years in the village of Exeter, and some of Daniel's siblings had attended. Daniel had preferred to be out hunting and fishing, and his parents never forced him to attend the school. "Let the girls do the spelling," his father often said, "and Daniel will do the shooting."

During the months after Samuel and Sarah's wedding, Daniel learned to read and write. It was not as difficult as he had imagined it to be, and he found it useful to be able to take notes about the wilderness areas where he hunted. He even tried his hand at making simple maps of where he hunted and found them useful, too.

Daniel's time of roaming the woods of Pennsylvania was quickly coming to an end, however. Ever since Daniel's father had been banned from Quaker meetings, he felt out of place in Exeter. By 1748 many Pennsylvania families were headed inland, to the Shenandoah Valley in the colony of Virginia.

It was a brave move to the frontier, fueled by promises of cheap, fertile land. The more Squire Boone discussed the idea of moving with his family, the more he liked it. Land in Pennsylvania was getting expensive, and since his married children wanted to stay close to their parents, things were getting a little too crowded.

Fourteen-year-old Daniel could hardly believe that his family might be moving west. He had heard that there were buffalo in Virginia, and he longed for a chance to practice his hunting skills on some of the land's most elusive game.

By May 1, 1750, all of the arrangements had been made. The homestead at Exeter had been sold to a distant relative for three hundred pounds, and Squire Boone had purchased all the necessary supplies the family would need for the trip west. The traveling party included Squire Boone and his wife, their eight unmarried children including Daniel, all three married children and their spouses, as well as Sarah and John's baby son, and Henry Miller, the apprentice.

Daniel was thrilled when the huge party finally got under way. He was fifteen now and was allowed to take his turn leading the packhorse train. He always had his rifle on hand, ready to pursue any worthy game he saw. He skillfully provided plenty of fresh meat for his family's entire traveling party.

Five horses were loaded up, and they covered fifteen miles a day. The route they took was well traveled with few real dangers. It took the group through the Cumberland Valley past several small towns, then farther down the valley, following the Yadkin River to Philadelphia Wagon road, and then through the Shenandoah Valley. The farther inland they traveled, the more exhilarated Daniel became. He could hardly wait for the new adventures that awaited him.

Chapter 4

On the Frontier

It was October 1751 before the Boone family finally settled on their own land. When they reached Virginia, they learned that land was even cheaper in the backwoods of North Carolina, where a square mile of land was selling for just three shillings. So the family had pressed on, and just before the first snow of winter arrived, Squire Boone purchased 640 acres of land in an area near the Yadkin River, located in what would become Rowan County, North Carolina.

As quickly as they could, the men in the Boone family banded together to build simple log cabins to shelter them through the winter. They had brought enough dry goods with them to last until their first harvest, but the group needed meat to help them survive. As soon as the roofs were on the cabins, Daniel was off hunting. He wanted to explore every inch of the land around him. The countryside was rolling and mostly wooded, broken occasionally by beautiful, broad meadows. Daniel learned that the local Catawba Indians had cleared many of these meadows, although the influx of new settlers had pushed the Catawba westward off much of their land.

The streams and rivers in the area flowed from the mountains and were clear and cold. Along their banks grew stands of native bamboo, which everyone called "cane." Much to Daniel's delight, the land teemed with wild animals to hunt such as buffalo, bears, wolves, deer, and turkeys. But with all the hunting going on in the area, it was not long before much of the game began to disappear.

The Boones were not the only family from Pennsylvania taking advantage of cheap land in North Carolina. Five years before, there had been only one hundred white men living in Rowan County and the adjoining two counties. But soon after the Boones' arrival, that number had shot up to three thousand men, in addition to the women and children. Most of them, like the Boone men, divided their time between planting and tending their corn crops and hunting in the backwoods. While the farming provided the families with food, it was the hunting that provided them with hard cash. Beaver-felt hats were the rage in Europe. As a result, beaver pelts were worth about forty cents a pound, or a dollar a pelt. At such prices, weight for weight, beaver skins were worth about five times as much as deerskin. Daniel hunted both animals. When he had accumulated a pile of pelts, he bundled them up and traded them for cash in the town of Salisbury.

Daniel much preferred hunting to farming. But as the oldest son still living at home, he was obliged to clear and plow land in the spring and plant the crops that would be harvested in the fall. As he worked, Daniel always hoped for rain. Farmwork stopped in the rain, and when it did, he would grab his rifle and head into the forest.

Within a year of arriving in North Carolina, Daniel had a reputation as a fine marksman. He hunted bears along a creek near the family's cabin, taking the meat home to his mother, who made enough jerky from it to feed the family for months.

The Boone family and their neighbors enjoyed the pioneering life. The land was fertile and yielded bountiful crops, just as the forests provided all the meat they could ever want. But in the summer of 1753, when Daniel was eighteen years old, a shadow settled over the western frontier. It came in the form of Indian attacks. These attacks were not from the local Catawba Indians but from tribes from the north. In fact, the Catawba sided with the settlers to fight off these roving bands.

In one skirmish a band of Shawnees attacked some isolated cabins not far from the Boone homestead. The local militia and the Catawbas fought back, killing several of the Shawnees. When the Shawnees' pouches were opened, they found silver crucifixes, beads, and mirrors, all made in France.

This discovery sent a ripple of terror through Rowan County. Daniel and everyone else knew exactly what it meant: The French government was supplying the Shawnee, Delaware, and Iroquois Indians with arms and trinkets to entice them to attack British settlers.

In the face of this, some families abandoned their farms, while the Boones and others who stayed tried to cope with the threat of attack as best they could.

In the fall of 1755, Daniel's younger sister Mary married William Bryan, the son of a wealthy landowner. It was a happy occasion, especially for Daniel, because at the wedding he was introduced to William's sixteen-year-old niece Rebecca Bryan. Rebecca was five feet three with long black hair and dark brown eyes. But it was not her looks that impressed Daniel as much as her behavior. Throughout the wedding feast, Rebecca was helpful and courteous to everyone around her. For the first time in his life, Daniel Boone found himself thinking about marriage.

The following spring Daniel and Rebecca joined a local group of young men and women who went on Saturday picnics together. Most of the others were engaged to be married, but Daniel was not sure how he could ever be positive that Rebecca was the right girl for him. That is, until he came up with a plan.

On one of their outings, Rebecca wore a new apron made of fine cambric, unlike most aprons, which were made of unbleached calico. Knowing that Rebecca was very proud of her fancy apron, Daniel used it to test her temper. As the two of them sat side by side eating a slice of pie, Daniel pulled his knife from its sheath, reached down, and cut several gashes in Rebecca's apron. On the last cut, he bumped Rebecca's leg so that she would look down and see what he was doing. The stunned Rebecca gave Daniel a puzzled look but did not say a word.

Daniel waited a few seconds, then smiled at her. "I'm sorry, but I had to do it," he apologized. "I wanted to see if you would fly into a rage or if you would wait to hear if I had an explanation for what I had done."

Rebecca slowly nodded her understanding. Although she did not look very pleased about what Daniel had done to her favorite apron, Daniel was very happy with how Rebecca reacted. He knew he could never marry a woman with a volatile temper, and now he was satisfied that Rebecca Bryan was as calm and serene on the inside as she looked on the outside. On the strength of a few cuts made in an apron, Daniel asked if he could officially court Rebecca, who, along with her family, agreed.

In the middle of their courting, however, the power struggle between Britain and France over control of the uncharted lands of North America erupted into a full-scale war. The focus of this conflict was over who controlled the confluence of the Monongahela and Allegheny Rivers, where they formed the Ohio River. The French, who had colonized eastern Canada, and the English each wanted to use the fork of the Ohio River as a base to push farther inland and claim more territory.

The settlers in North Carolina were powerless to do anything but listen to rumors about who had gained control of what. In 1754 Daniel learned that the French had built Fort Duquesne at the fork of the Ohio River, and an up-and-coming young Virginian named George Washington had led a force of men to overrun the fort and claim it for Virginia. After Colonel Washington and his men had been repelled by the French, the British decided to send a much larger force, consisting of two regiments under the leadership of General Edward Braddock, to undertake the task. This force's mission was to drive the French back into Canada and secure the Ohio River for the British.

Before the troops marched for Fort Duquesne, a call went out for local farmers with good rifle skills to join the battle. Despite his Quaker upbringing, in which men were taught not to go to war, Daniel Boone signed up. He could not simply sit by and watch the French and their Indian allies take over the western frontier, nor could he turn down the opportunity for an adventure.

Daniel was assigned as a wagon driver for a unit led by Major Edward Dobbs, the son of the governor of North Carolina. In May the frontiersmen marched north to Fort Cumberland in western Maryland. Not long after they arrived, General Braddock's British regular soldiers arrived. The stage was set for the attack on Fort Duquesne, one hundred miles to the west.

In early June 1755 nearly two thousand men set out to attack the French and Indians. The column of men and supply wagons stretched for nearly four miles as they made their way across the mountains. At the front of the column, axmen chopped away at trees and bushes on either side of the old Indian trail they followed. Other men then removed the stumps and formed a road wide enough for the cannons and supply wagons.

After a week of slogging through the mountains the force had covered only thirty miles. General Braddock was frustrated by the slow progress and split his army in two. Most of the heavy supplies were left with the rear army, while the faster group pushed forward, their supplies loaded on packhorses and wagons whose loads had been greatly lightened to speed them along. Yet it still took them three more weeks to get to their destination.

Daniel drove one of the wagons in the faster group. At night, as the men camped along the trail, Daniel made friends with another wagon driver named John Findley. John had been born in Ireland and had come to the new land in 1722 with his parents. Like Daniel he had been raised in Pennsylvania. The two men would sit by the campfire and talk about their adventures on the frontier. John had been farther afield than Daniel, as far away as Kentucky, and he regaled Daniel with stories of his adventures there. He made the place sound like a paradise.

"The land is all cane and clover, with beautiful fertile valleys," John told Daniel. "A man can get enough land for himself, his children, and his grandchildren. And the wild game there is beyond belief. Every imaginable animal wanders in the forest and on the grassy plains," he continued. "A man will never want for fresh meat in Kentucky. And if that were not enough, the current at the falls of the Ohio is so strong that plump ducks and geese are every day washed over it onto the rocks below. A man does not even need a gun to catch his food there. All he needs to do is go to the bottom of the falls and collect his fill to cook."

Daniel's eyes sparkled as he listened to John talk.

"To get to this unequaled land from North Carolina, boy," John told Daniel, "go in a northwesterly direction and penetrate Cumberland Mountain at the great gap. From there you follow the ancient Warrior's Path to the land I speak of."

Daniel nodded quietly and stored away the information about Kentucky that John had given him. The place fascinated him, and he decided that when the war with the French was over, he would see it for himself.

On July 9 the British force crossed the Monongahela River. They were just twelve miles from Fort Duquesne. By 2:30 in the afternoon, they were seven miles from the fort. From his vantage point on the wagon at the back of the force, Daniel took in the sight. British soldiers clad in red coats and tan breeches marched in exact formation. Behind them came Virginia militiamen dressed in blue tunics, and behind them colonial volunteers from the other colonies. General Braddock did not trust the colonial soldiers' will to fight and had ordered them to the rear of the formation. The sound of fifes and drums filled the air as officers mounted on horses barked out orders. The polished rifles of the soldiers gleamed in the afternoon sun as the soldiers wound their way along the trail that ran through thick woods with a hill rising on one side.

When Daniel heard the shots, his wagon loaded with food supplies was a half mile behind the lead group of soldiers. The shots were sporadic at first, but then a sustained volley opened up. The air quickly filled with the acrid smell of gunpowder as British soldiers began to fall. It soon became clear that the soldiers from Fort Duquesne and their Indian allies had ambushed General Braddock's army.

The colonial soldiers dispersed to fight in the woods, but the British officers demanded that their men stay in formation. But in formation the men were easy targets for the unseen enemy hidden in the thick forest cover. Daniel watched in horror as line after line of British soldiers fell dead. A British officer galloped up and ordered the wagon drivers to hold their positions, ready to advance. Daniel obeyed, but as the mayhem ahead of them continued, many drivers cut their horses free and fled, leaving their laden wagons in the middle of the trail.

As more British soldiers rushed forward to engage the enemy, they ran into other soldiers trying to flee the battle. In their terror the British began firing on each other. The discipline of the battlefield had completely broken down. From General Braddock galloped back and forth, barking orders and trying to regain control of his army. The officers mounted on horses were easy targets for the French and Indians, and as more and more officers were shot, the mayhem of the battlefield grew. All seemed hopeless. But one officer caught Daniel's attention. He was Colonel George Washington of Virginia. He seemed fearless in the face of the fighting as he tried to calm the soldiers' fears and urge them forward. When Washington's horse was shot out from under him, Colonel Washington simply found another horse that had lost its rider, swung himself up onto the animal, and went right back to trying to rally the troops.

After three hours of fighting, hundreds of British soldiers were either dead or writhing in pain. And when General Braddock was shot and fell from his horse seriously wounded, the soldiers had had enough. They began breaking rank and fleeing back to the river. As they pushed past his supply wagon, Daniel decided it was time for him to flee as well. He leaped onto his lead horse, cut it free from the harness, and galloped off toward the Monongahela River.

When totals were tallied from Braddock's Defeat, as it became known, nine hundred of the fourteen hundred British soldiers were either dead or missing. General Braddock himself lay dead, and George Washington had emerged as the colonial hero.

Thankful that his life had been spared, Daniel made his way back to North Carolina and thought about what he would do next. Two things kept crossing his mind: marrying Rebecca Bryan and exploring the land of Kentucky. John Findley's description of the place still burned in Daniel's mind, but Daniel's affection for Rebecca burned in his heart. Daniel began to wonder whether he could both marry Rebecca and explore the Kentucky territory. Or would he have to sacrifice one so that he could pursue the other?

Chapter 5

Unsettled Times

On his arrival back in North Carolina, Daniel found that he had more pressing things to think about than asking Mr. Bryan for his daughter's hand in marriage. His older brother Israel was ill with tuberculosis. A week before Daniel got home, Israel's wife had died of the disease. It was a sad situation, as there seemed little hope for Israel and his family of four young children. Daniel helped his mother take Israel to the Moravian hospital in the newly established town of Salem, but sadly, Israel died, leaving two daughters and two sons without parents. Daniel thought the situation over. Family members would rear the girls, while Daniel would not only ask Rebecca to marry him but also ask her to help him raise the boys.

Happily Rebecca agreed to both requests, and she and Daniel set August 14, 1756, as the date for their wedding. Daniel's father, who was a justice of the peace, would officiate.

The wedding was a grand affair, since Rebecca's grandfather, Morgan Bryan, had been one of the original landholders in North Carolina and became very wealthy as a result of land deals. As was traditional, seventeen-year-old Rebecca brought many items with her to the wedding. Her dowry of linens, furniture, and cooking equipment was displayed for all the guests to see.

Daniel and Rebecca did not have time for a honeymoon. They had crops to harvest and Jesse and Jonathan to care for. At first the new family of four lived in a cabin on Squire Boone's property. Within months they moved to Sugar Tree Creek, a part of Rebecca's father's settlement, where Daniel's sisters Elizabeth and Mary already lived with their husbands.

Daniel and Rebecca busied themselves making a home. They built a roomy log cabin and cleared land for a small farm. But as they worked, they worried about being attacked by hostile Indians. Soon, Governor Dobbs ordered that a series of forts be built along the western border of North Carolina. Whenever the alarm of an impending attack sounded, Rebecca and the children would head for the safety of the fort while Daniel would grab his rifle and join the local militia to hunt for the attackers. As word spread that the western frontier was becoming more dangerous, gangs of white bandits flooded into the area to take advantage of the turmoil. In the midst of this, Rebecca Boone gave birth to their first baby, a son whom they named James. A second son, Israel, quickly followed.

By 1759 the attacks had become frequent and fierce. Shawnee warriors from Ohio swept down and raided the border between North Carolina and Virginia, burning fields, stealing supplies, and murdering anyone who got in their way. The Indians were not the only ones creating mayhem. A group of settlers passing through the area kidnapped and scalped some warriors. This was all part of the French and Indian war, which had begun at Fort Duquesne.

In February 1760 Cherokee warriors killed a number of Daniel's neighbors in the Yadkin settlement. Like most other men in Yadkin, Daniel felt it was time to pack up his family and leave. Some of Daniel's brothers and sisters had already left, and in March the remaining Boone clan headed northeast.

As his family pushed along the grueling trail, Daniel could not help thinking about the house and belongings he'd had to leave behind, and he wondered when he would get to see his land again. It was not easy for Rebecca either. She had four young children to watch over, and she was expecting another baby in late autumn.

The packhorse train headed along the Georgia Road, a trail that took them past the Moravian village of Bethania and through Lynchburg. Two hundred miles after setting out, they arrived in

Culpepper County, Virginia. Because there were no woods in which to hunt, Daniel hauled tobacco in Culpepper County to raise money to support his family. This new life did not suit Daniel one bit.

Baby Susannah Boone was born on November 2, 1760, and soon after her arrival Daniel decided to return to the backwoods of North Carolina to hunt. He longed to be back in the wilderness; trading and selling pelts would be a much more agreeable way for him to earn an income.

When Daniel passed through the settlement at Yadkin, he found it largely abandoned. Militiamen from Virginia were in the area, invading Cherokee towns and killing anyone who did not flee fast enough. Daniel was glad that his family was far away from the gruesome activities of both sides.

One cold night Daniel sat alone beside a campfire. Next to him was a large bundle of beaver pelts he was taking to the trading post. Suddenly he heard a twig snap. He was instantly alert, but it was too late. Eight Indian warriors stepped into the firelight. "Ah, we've got you now, Widemouth!" one of them exclaimed.

Daniel took a deep breath. He knew it would be a fatal mistake to show any sign of fear. "Welcome," he said, slowly reaching for his knapsack. "I have plenty of jerky. Would you like to share some with me?"

The lead Indian looked surprised. He was still for a moment; then he laid down his rifle and laughed. "You have the courage of a bear," he said. "We shall spare your life but take your furs. And tell your white friends that you are all intruding on our hunting grounds and killing all of our game. Leave here, and don't come back."

Daniel decided to keep his mouth shut and offer the warriors more jerky, which they accepted. Ten minutes later they disappeared into the darkness along with all his beaver pelts, the product of two weeks of hunting. Still, Daniel was grateful that his life had been spared. These days many hunters did not return from Cherokee country.

After his pelts were taken, Daniel set out to hunt more beaver, determined that despite the Cherokees' warning, he would take money back to Rebecca and the children. When he finally did make it back to Virginia, Daniel continued to take long hunting trips to North Carolina, which supplied him with plenty of the valuable pelts to sell and enabling him to meet all of his family's financial needs.

By end of 1762, Daniel returned to his house at Sugar Tree Creek, planting a crop of wheat and rye before returning to Virginia to collect his family. It was a joyous trip back to North Carolina for the Boone family. Baby Susannah sat in an Indian-style sling on Rebecca's back the entire way, while Israel and James doubled up on a horse. The rest of the extended Boone family followed a month later.

Back in Yadkin the Boones were greeted by many of their old neighbors who had already returned to resume their pioneer lives. A new Boone baby was born as well, named Jemima. The Boones now had two boys and two girls, plus Daniel's nephews to take care of.

Now that the Indian wars were over in the region, hundreds of other white people surged into the area. Just as the Boones had been over ten years before, they were eager to buy land and build cabins. Within a year after the Boones' return, Rowan County was booming. Yadkin was no longer a tiny settlement but a thriving township. This posed a problem for Daniel, who preferred to make his living by hunting, as did many of the newcomers. Each time he hunted, Daniel noticed that there was less game in the area.

As far as Daniel was concerned, it was time to pick up everything and move west again. He told Rebecca that he wanted the family to pioneer a homestead in the high meadows of the Blue Ridge Mountains. Daniel picked out a site that he thought was perfect. It was right near the Proclamation Line of 1763, and the British government had guaranteed the Indians that no homes or settlements would be built beyond it. Daniel was convinced that the area around the line would never become too crowded. There was just one problem with Daniel's plan. As mild tempered as Rebecca was, she had a stubborn streak and refused to consider moving into the wilderness again. Daniel was left to think of another way to escape the "crowds."

In the meantime Daniel hunted farther afield than he had before, bringing home meat and money from the sale of furs and skins. When his oldest son, James, turned seven, Daniel began taking him on some of his shorter hunting trips. The young boy loved it, even when it snowed heavily and the two of them were tucked in blankets under a thick layer of snow. Daniel showed James how to recognize various tracks and how to take his bearing from the sun and the wind so that he would never be lost in the wilderness.

On January 2, 1765, Daniel learned that his father had died. The news came as a shock, because the last time he had seen his father he appeared fit and healthy. Burial arrangements were made, and Squire Boone was buried the following day. Daniel's mother went to live with Daniel's sister Mary and her family.

After his father's funeral, Daniel felt very alone. He was thirty years old, and he was restless. He could not imagine living out the rest of his life in and around Yadkin. He knew he needed another adventure, and that adventure presented itself when five of his friends from Culpepper County, Virginia, showed up on Daniel's doorstep.

The five men were on their way to explore the territory of Florida. This new territory had been added to the British domain in North America with England's victory over France and Spain. To attract colonists to Florida, the British government was offering one hundred acres of free land to anyone who would settle in the territory. Daniel's ears pricked up at the talk of free land, and he decided to accompany the five on their trip. His brother Squire and his sister Hannah's husband, John Stuart, also decided to go along.

Daniel kissed Rebecca good-bye and promised he would be back in time to eat Christmas dinner with her and the children. Then the eight men mounted their horses and headed for Florida. The route they followed took them south to Ninety-Six, the largest settlement on the Carolina frontier. From there they made their way to Savannah, Georgia, where they picked up the Old King's Road and followed it to Saint Augustine, Florida.

Florida, however, was not the kind of wilderness Daniel had expected. Instead of rolling grassland and forests to hunt in, most of Florida seemed to Daniel to be one big swamp. And if that were not enough, the place swarmed with bugs. No matter how hard they tried, the men could not seem to get away from mosquitoes that bit them mercilessly.

From Saint Augustine the group headed west to the St. Johns River, where they hoped to hunt game. Unfortunately, by the time they left the St. Johns behind, they had little to show for all their effort. Daniel was surprised at just how little game there seemed to be in Florida.

As they headed toward Pensacola, in the extreme western corner of the panhandle of Florida, Daniel's brother-in-law John became separated from the group. He finally caught up to the others five days later, half-starved and terrified that he was going to die in the Florida wilderness and that his body would never be found. His anxiety was not put to rest when several days later the whole group became lost in a swamp. For three days they trudged in circles through knee-deep mud, avoiding the predatory jaws of the alligators and searching for deer for food. As the men and their horses reached the exhaustion point, they encountered a group of Seminole Indians. The Seminoles were friendly and led the men out of the swamp to their nearby village. They fed the men deer and wild honey, which the men, none of whom had eaten during their ordeal in the swamp, gulped down.

Daniel was fascinated by how well the Seminoles' village was suited to the environment. The village was located on a sandy knoll above the high-water mark of the surrounding swamp. The floors of the Seminoles' houses were set about two feet off the ground. Each structure was mostly open sided, with six poles supporting a roof made of thatched palmetto fronds. As he lay down to sleep in one of the small houses that night, Daniel realized just how ingenious the design was. Not only was he sleeping on a high and dry platform, but also the elevated floor allowed the gentle evening breezes to swish through the house, keeping the occupants cool.

The following morning the group once again set out for Pensacola, and several days later, much to Daniel's delight, the small community came into view.

Although Florida was entirely different from what he had imagined, Daniel found that the warm, untamed territory appealed to his sense of adventure. He even grew to like the town of

Pensacola, which was located on a bay and protected from the open ocean by a barrier island. Cool breezes blew in from the bay, and the streets of the town were neatly laid out. In fact, Daniel liked the place so much that he decided to buy a tract of land in town, on which he intended to build a house, and move Rebecca and the children from North Carolina.

After their stay in Pensacola, it was time for the men to head north for home. They headed through the territory of the Creek Indians (Alabama) before crossing into Georgia. They traversed South Carolina, and on Christmas Day Daniel finally arrived home, just in time to eat Christmas dinner with his family as he had promised.

After an enthusiastic welcome, Daniel sat down beside Rebecca. As they ate, he excitedly told his wife about Florida, the good and the bad, and about the land he had bought in Pensacola and how he intended to move the family there as soon as he had built a house on the lot.

"I will do nothing of the sort," Rebecca retorted when she heard her husband's plan for the family. "I tell you, Daniel Boone, you cannot expect me to move so far away from all my family and friends. I simply will not move to Pensacola."

Daniel sat stunned. He had not expected this reaction from Rebecca. But her mind was made up, and Daniel knew when that happened, there was no way to change it. There would be no house in Pensacola, no further exploration of Florida's swampy jungles. Daniel would have to come up with another plan, but what could it be? He began to despair of ever living the adventurous life he had dreamed of as a boy.

Chapter 6

Kentucky at Last

The following year, 1766, Daniel did manage to convince Rebecca to make a move. It was not nearly as far as he would have liked, but it was a move nonetheless. Rebecca agreed mainly because other members of Daniel's family, including his brothers George, Edward, and Squire and his sister Hannah and her husband, John, all sold their land and were preparing to move as well.

Daniel and Rebecca and their family, which now included a baby girl named Levina, ventured sixty-five miles up the Yadkin River to Holman's Ford, an untamed area in the lower reaches of the Brushy Mountains of North Carolina. The following year the family moved twice more, until they settled several more miles upriver where Beaver Creek flowed into the Yadkin.

The various branches of the Boone family helped each other to build log cabins in which to spend the winter, and in spring they cleared land on which to plant crops. Daniel was happy again. He told his brothers that he never wanted to live in a cabin where he had to walk more than one hundred feet to fell a tree. For now, he had his wish. The children were growing fast. Daniel's nephew Jonathan was now seventeen, and Daniel's oldest son James was ten years old. Since there was no school in the area, the children spent most of the day helping with chores, which freed Daniel to go hunting in the foothills of the Blue Ridge Mountains. During the fall and winter, Daniel hunted for turkeys, beaver, bears, and deer. But during the summer he hunted for something quite different, a root called ginseng.

Ginseng was a sought-after natural medicine in the colonies and as far away as China. It grew wild in the mountains of North Carolina, and nearly all of the pioneers in the foothills searched for it. Daniel proved to be one of the best "root" hunters. He used a method that enabled him to collect twice as much ginseng as anyone else. He carried a small leather bag with him, and when it was full, he emptied its contents onto the ground and went in search of more of the root. At the end of the day, he would take a couple of his children back to all the spots where he had left piles of roots, and they would bring it all home. Unlike most others who tried this method, Daniel never forgot where he left his piles of ginseng. The collected roots were then sold to merchants located along the Atlantic coast who shipped them off to the Orient.

The "backcountry" of North Carolina was becoming dangerous once again. In the spring of 1767, a raiding party of northern Indians attacked a party of five traders traveling down the Tennessee River. All of the traders were killed in the skirmish that followed. When news of the incident reached Daniel and his neighbors, the men went out to bury the bodies of the traders. It was a sobering sight when they reached the place of the attack, but it did not deter Daniel from his determination to explore new places.

As the winter of 1767 approached, Daniel's thoughts turned westward toward Kentucky, or Kanta-ke, as the Iroquois Indians had named the land. Somehow John Findley's description of the country west of the Appalachians and south of the Ohio River still lingered in Daniel's mind. He was determined to go and see the place for himself, and in late fall Daniel, his brother Squire, and his friend William Hill set off up the Clinch River. At the source of the river, they crossed the ridge of the Appalachian Mountains and headed down the other side. Because there were no maps of the area, they had to guess what lay ahead. Eventually they emerged from the mountains on the other side. The only problem was that everything was covered with several feet of snow. Daniel had not realized just how bitter the winter could be on the far side of the Appalachians. The group was soon mired down in the snow. Storm after storm swept across the foothills, making it impossible to travel any distance.

Daniel and the others realized they would not see much of Kentucky in this weather, and they reluctantly decided to spend the winter in the foothills. They found a bubbling spring that did not freeze and set up camp nearby. Each man took turns hunting for food, but this was not an arduous task. Buffalo and deer came regularly to drink at the spring, and all the men had to do was aim their rifles and shoot. Daniel and the others spent the winter feasting on roast rump of buffalo and deer tenderloin.

Despite the abundance of meat through the winter, the spring thaw could not come fast enough for the men. As soon as it arrived, the men broke camp and headed home, back across the mountains to North Carolina, leaving most of Kentucky—still buried under many feet of snow—unexplored.

When Daniel arrived back home, he found North Carolina buzzing with controversy over taxation. The farmers around Yadkin and other small towns in North Carolina felt that they were underrepresented in the colony's government and were being asked to pay too many taxes and fees. This mirrored a growing sentiment in many of the other colonies as well. Colonists, many of whose parents, and even grandparents and great-grandparents, had been born on colonial American soil were being asked to pay ever larger amounts of taxes to the British government. The people of North Carolina began to protest. Many joined a group called the Regulators, who took it upon themselves to rise up against merchants who charged the various taxes and fees required by the British government. Although the Regulators used peaceful methods of protest against "the lawyers who practice numberless devilish devices to rob us of our livings," Daniel had a feeling things could turn violent if the governor of the colony did not reconsider his harsh stand on taxation.

All of this political turmoil simply added to Daniel's resolve to get out of the crowded settlements and deeper into the wilderness. If Kentucky was indeed the paradise that John Findley had described, he wanted to be there.

Just as the first snow of winter 1768 began to fall, Daniel discovered that his dream was closer at hand than he imagined. A peddler and horse dealer knocked on the door of the Boone cabin, and Daniel immediately recognized the man's Irish lilt. It was John Findley! The two men had not seen each other in thirteen years.

That evening, and for many evenings afterward, Daniel, his brothers and sons, and John sat around the fire swapping stories of what they knew or had heard about the western lands. John brought news of the Treaty of Fort Stanwix, in which the Iroquois ceded vast amounts of land in Kentucky to the British. Daniel was sure that the way was open for him to make a more thorough visit to the area.

As they discussed such a venture, John convinced Daniel that it would be unsafe to retrace the route he had taken with his brother Squire and William Hill the previous winter. Too many hostile Indians were situated along Boone's original route. Instead, John proposed they cross the mountains farther to the south, in the Ouasioto or Cumberland Range. Daniel eagerly agreed to this and promised that when he crossed the mountains this time, he would have all the equipment and traveling companions he needed. He planned to make a general survey of the land beyond the mountains and bring back a full report of what he found.

Daniel knew he did not have enough money to equip such an expedition, and neither did John Findley. The two of them set about finding someone to finance their trip. It did not take long to interest an attorney named Richard Henderson in financing the scheme. In exchange for information that could lead to settlements sometime in the future, Henderson would pay for their trip. Throughout the winter of 1768, Daniel and John made lists of everything they would need to take with them when they set off the following spring. Their plan was to leave as soon as the spring crops were planted, and they would collect animal skins along the way to sell.

To accompany them on the trip, Daniel recruited his sister Hannah's husband, John Stuart, as well as three neighbors, Joseph Holder, James Mooney, and Bill Cooley. His brother Squire offered to stay behind and watch over the wives, children, and farms of the adventurers.

On the morning of May 1, 1769, Daniel kissed his wife and the children—including newborn daughter Rebecca—good-bye. His sister Hannah was there also to bid her husband farewell, and Daniel promised to bring John back safely and as soon as possible.

The men were clad in frontiersmen dress. This consisted of a loose, open shirt made of deerskin, deerskin leggings, and moccasins. Around their waist was a heavy leather belt from which hung a tomahawk, a hunting knife in a sheath, a powder horn, and a bullet pouch. Most of the men wore fur caps, many made from raccoon pelts, but Daniel did not like such caps and never wore them. He preferred to wear a plain hat.

Daniel's mind whirled with both uncertainty and the expectation of adventure as the men mounted their horses and headed off to the south. The men took with them ten packhorses, onto whose backs were piled the supplies they would need for the trip. These included such things as camp kettles, blankets, some food items such as flour, ground corn, and salt, extra gunpowder, and lead, plus the tools to turn the lead into bullets, as well as flints and tinder to start their campfires.

Over the next five weeks, the slow journey took the men across the Blue Ridge Mountains, over Stone Mountain, through Moccasin Gap, and over Powell Mountain and Wallen's Ridge. In the valley of the Powell River, they encountered twenty men led by Joseph Martin of Virginia. These men were attempting to build a small settlement in the valley. It was the most westerly settlement on the frontier, and Daniel promised to return and visit them on his way back to North Carolina.

From the Powell River, they made their way to the Cumberland Gap, which bisected the tall, white cliffs of the Cumberland Mountains. Having passed through the gap, they followed the Cumberland River southward until they reached the foothills beyond which lay Kentucky. Daniel was awed by what he saw as he stood on a high rock overlooking the plains. Herds of buffalo nibbled at the bluegrass that covered the plain, while ducks and geese flew over the cane swaths that bordered the rivers and streams. Once in Kentucky, the men came to a hospitable-looking creek and set up a camp, which they called Station Camp.

Daniel and his traveling companions took full advantage of the sunny skies and the abundance of wild animals to hunt. For the next six months they hunted and trapped every day. Two of the men always stayed back at Station Camp to clean the deerskins from the day before and pack them up and hoist them onto scaffolds to keep them away from bears and wolves.

It was an idyllic life for Daniel, who had the chance to live outdoors and explore new land every day. Although the men kept an eye out for Indians, they never saw any, and Daniel wondered whether they would get through the trip without any difficulties with the Indians. At least he wondered that until he had a disturbing dream just before Christmas.

Chapter 7

A Bad Dream

On the night of December 22, 1769, Daniel dreamed that he saw his father walking toward him. Daniel held out his hand to welcome him, but his father pushed it away angrily. Daniel awoke deeply disturbed. In the past he had noticed that when he had a dream in which his father was happy, things went well. But when he dreamed that his father was angry, danger lay ahead. In this dream, Daniel's father was very unhappy.

A sense of dread hung over Daniel as he and John Stuart spent the following day hunting. When they were on their way back to camp in late afternoon, Daniel heard a war whoop and then the hiss of a tomahawk as it flew through the air and landed beside him. Fifteen Shawnee warriors burst out from a stand of cane, and in an instant the two white men were surrounded. Daniel grabbed John's arm and whispered to him, "Stand still. I will do the talking."

Using the pidgin Indian language he had picked up on various hunting trips, Daniel tried to reason with the Shawnees. Their leader was a man named Captain Will, and he was not interested in talk. He made it clear that what he wanted was to be led to Station Camp and nothing else would satisfy him.

Realizing that he had no choice but to take them, Daniel set out first for several of the smaller camps they had set up in the area. As he went, he made as much noise as possible, hoping that some of the other members of his hunting party would hear them and remove the horses and skins from Station Camp before he led the Shawnee warriors there.

His plan half worked. By the time he led the warriors into Station Camp, the rest of the men had fled into the forest, but they had not taken any of the horses, supplies, or skins with them. Daniel felt sick when he and John were forced to help load the skins onto their own horses for the Indians to take. The pelts were worth at least a thousand dollars. Even divided five ways, it would still have left a tidy sum of money that Daniel had intended to take home with him.

When the skins were tied down onto the horses, Captain Will ordered his braves to go through the camp looking for guns, ammunition, and anything else that struck their fancy. The items they found were then wrapped in skins and secured to the horses with straps of buffalo hide.

When nothing of value was left in the camp, Captain Will ordered his warriors to mount their horses. As they did so, he pulled some things from the saddlebag on his horse. "Here, take these," he said, throwing down four pairs of moccasins, two small French guns, gunpowder, and lead. "Now, brothers," he continued, "go home and stay there. Do not come back here anymore, for this is our hunting ground. The British made a treaty with the Iroquois, but we hunt here, and we had no part of the treaty. All the animals, skins, and furs here belong to us. If you are foolish enough to come back again, you may be sure the wasps and yellow jackets will sting you severely."

Before Daniel could think of a reply, Captain Will had mounted his horse and signaled the Indians forward. Daniel and John watched helplessly as the fruit of six months of hunting and trapping disappeared into the forest.

It was too much for Daniel to bear. "Quick," he said, grabbing the guns Captain Will had thrown down and tucking one into his belt. "Let's go after them."

"On foot?" his brother-in-law inquired.

"Yes. We have to try to catch them. The horses are so heavily laden with our skins they'll be going slowly, and they probably won't travel at night. Come on. Get some jerky and let's go."

"But shouldn't we wait for the others?"

Daniel shook his head. "I want our skins back, and the sooner we get going, the better."

With that Daniel marched off in the direction the horses had gone. John followed close behind. The two men did not rest until sunset, when they stopped to eat some jerky and wild grapes. As they ate, they considered their next step.

"The only way we can get our horses and skins back is to creep into the camp at night and hope the guard is asleep. There's no way we can overpower them during the daylight, especially since they'll be on horseback," Daniel said.

John agreed, and when their simple meal was over, the two men crept on, aware that the Shawnees were probably not far ahead.

Sure enough, they discovered the Shawnees encamped a short distance away. They waited for several minutes and spied on the camp. When Daniel was sure all the warriors were asleep, he signaled for John to follow him. They wouldn't be able to retrieve both the horses and all the skins at once, but getting their horses back would be a good start. Keeping low, the two men sneaked over to where the horses were tied up. They noiselessly untied the animals and led them out of the camp. When Daniel was satisfied they were far enough from the camp and that the Indians were still sleeping, he whispered to John to mount up. Each man swung himself up onto the back of a horse and galloped toward Station Camp.

Daniel and John rode on through the night, and as the early morning sun began to peek over the eastern mountains, Daniel decided it was time to stop and rest. He dismounted and fell onto his back in the long grass on the gently sloping meadow. He was enjoying the warmth of the sun on his face when he became aware of the ground thundering beneath him. He looked up just in time to see Captain Will and his band of warriors gallop into view. It was too late for Daniel and John to mount their horses and ride off, and for the second time in two days, Daniel Boone had been captured by Indians.

One of the warriors rode up and looked down at Daniel. "Steal horse, ha?" he snarled in broken English. Then he reached over and placed a horse collar lined with little bells around Daniel's neck. "Dance," he commanded, leveling his rifle at Daniel.

Daniel began shuffling his feet while the Indians roared with laughter. When they had finished their fun, the Shawnees tied Daniel and John together and took them with them. Captain Will explained that once the Shawnees were safely across the Ohio River with their stolen booty, the two white men would be let go.

Daniel was determined to get away before he got as far as the Ohio. During the seven days it took to reach the banks of the river, he worked nonstop on an escape plan. As Captain Will and his party finalized their strategy for crossing the river, Daniel managed at last to snap the strip of hide that bound him and his brother-in-law together. The two men took several rifles and some ammunition and fled into a dense stand of cane nearby.

To avoid being recaptured, the two men hid in the canebrake until the Indians gave up looking for them and resumed their preparations for crossing the Ohio River. Daniel knew that Captain Will could easily have set the cane on fire and forced them out. But the Indian leader had said he intended the men no harm, and by his actions Daniel knew that he meant it.

Once the Shawnees were on the other side of the river, Daniel and John started back to their camp. When they reached Station Camp, they found it abandoned. Daniel realized that the other four men had probably given up hope of ever seeing them again and set out for North Carolina. It took Daniel and John two more days' walking to catch up to them. The men were shocked to see them alive. They were sure the Shawnees had killed them.

After the frustration and humiliation of having the hides and most of their belongings stolen, a pleasant surprise awaited Daniel. His brother Squire and a neighbor named Alexander Neeley had joined the other four men. Unable to contain his curiosity as to what Kentucky was like, Squire had set out with horses and extra supplies to find Daniel. He bore the news that Cherokees had broken up Joseph Martin's settlement in the Powell River Valley. The settlement had not even lasted long enough to harvest the first crop of corn the men had planted. Squire also told Daniel the exciting news that Rebecca was expecting another baby soon. Daniel was delighted.

The horses and supplies Squire had brought with him were a welcome sight, and they gave Daniel fresh hope. Now the men did not have to walk back to North Carolina after all; they could turn around and go back to Station Camp and do more hunting and exploring.

The idea of going back to Station Camp was not well received by John Findley, Joseph Holder, James Mooney, and Bill Cooley. Considering themselves lucky to have escaped Kentucky with their lives, they would not turn around. Squire Boone and Alexander Neeley, on the other hand, were eager to see Kentucky for themselves. It was agreed that the four men would head back over the mountains on foot and return home while Daniel and John Stuart took the horses and led Squire and Alexander back into Kentucky.

At Station Camp the men were able to salvage several pots and some harnesses. They then moved several miles to the northwest, to a spot near the site of an abandoned Indian settlement called Blue Lick Town.

The weather warmed slightly, and the men were able to hunt buffalo and trap beaver. They named various creeks and hills as they passed by them; Daniel even named one creek Lulbegrud after the capital city of the giants in *Gulliver's Travels*. By late winter Daniel was pleased with the group's success after the theft. The four men, divided into pairs, were an efficient team, and the beaver were plentiful. Daniel's optimism, however, was soon crushed.

One morning in early spring, Daniel and John split up, each man going down one side of the Kentucky River checking on beaver traps. The river was swollen from rain and melting snow, and the current was swift. When Daniel had finished checking his traps, he waited for John, but John did not appear. Assuming that his brother-in-law had decided not to risk crossing the river in flood, Daniel returned to camp for the night.

Another day went by, and then another, and still Daniel thought John was cautiously waiting on the other side of the river for the waters to subside. On the third day, when the river finally did go down, John failed to show up. Daniel crossed the river to search for him. He found John's makeshift camp but no sign of John. Although Daniel and the other two men searched for days, they could not figure out what had happened to the fourth member of their party. They had no way of knowing whether John had been captured by Indians or had drowned trying to cross the river. Daniel dreaded carrying the news of John's disappearance back to Hannah.

Alexander became so spooked by John's disappearance that he wanted to get out of Kentucky and back into civilization as fast as possible. He decided to return to North Carolina, leaving the Boone brothers, probably the only white men in the region, alone in Kentucky. If anything happened to them, there was little chance that anyone could come to their rescue.

By May 1770 Daniel and Squire felt they had collected and dressed enough beaver and deer skins to make a trip back over the Appalachian Mountains to the nearest trading post to sell them. They decided that Squire should make the trip alone while Daniel stayed in Kentucky exploring farther west.

While his brother was away, Daniel explored along many uncharted streams, sleeping each night in stands of cane for protection. He never slept in the same place twice lest any Indians were trailing him and might attack him during the night. In the day he hunted and would start a fire around noon and cook venison or buffalo to eat. Then, later in the afternoon, he would explore further before finding a canebrake in which to spend the night.

On July 28 Daniel returned to the Blue Lick camp to find that Squire had arrived there a day earlier. It was a happy reunion, especially when Daniel heard from his brother that Daniel's family was doing well. Rebecca had given birth to another boy, who was named Daniel Morgan after his father.

Because Daniel was assured that his family at home was safe, he felt comfortable staying in Kentucky to hunt through another summer and fall. He and Squire collected a huge pile of hides, and by February 1771 Daniel was ready and eager to return to Rebecca and the children.

The two brothers tied the skins into bundles and broke camp. They headed east through the Cumberland Gap and camped in the Powell River Valley, as Daniel had done on the way to Kentucky twenty-one months before.

While camped in the Powell River Valley, the Boone brothers went hunting. It was midafternoon, and they were about to head back to camp when in the distance they spotted a white man. They caught up to the man, and when he spoke, they realized it was their hunting companion Alexander Neeley. But how his appearance had changed. He was gaunt, his eyes were sunken, and his body was filthy. His clothes were now just tattered rags, and he had cuts all over his legs and arms.

Alexander was overjoyed to see them. They sat down together on a log, and Alexander poured out his tale of woe. He had come with a party of hunters to hunt near the Cumberland Gap, when he was separated from the others. He searched desperately for the men, and when he did not find them, he fired off shot after shot from his rifle, hoping the sound would lead the others to him. It did not, and soon Alexander had used up all his gunpowder. For several more days, he wandered, trying to find their camp, but only ended up more lost. He gave up hope of being found and began to wander aimlessly in the wilderness.

With no gun to catch food, hunger soon overcame him, and he started to get delirious. When one day a friendly dog bounded up to him, Alexander was not sure at first whether the animal was real or just some wishful invention of his deranged mind. But when he reached out to pat the animal, he realized it was real and instinct took over. Alexander pulled out his knife and killed the animal. After skinning the dog, he started a fire and roasted it. After he had eaten, he made a bag from the dogskin and put the leftover meat into it. He had kept wandering for several more days, eating a little of the leftover dog meat each day, until he stumbled upon the Boone brothers.

Daniel and Squire immediately took Alexander back to their camp to feed and clothe him. As they set out toward camp, Alexander, who had given up hope of being rescued and was prepared to die alone in the wilderness, pulled the dog meat from his bag and threw it onto the ground. "I won't be needing this anymore," he said.

After several days at camp and many meals of roast venison and buffalo rump, Alexander regained his strength. Daniel gave him a horse and gun and showed him the trail he needed to follow to catch up to the rest of his hunting party.

After Alexander left them, the Boone brothers made their way further along the Powell River Valley, where they again camped. One night as they sat around the fire at their new campsite, a group of eight Indians suddenly appeared out of the darkness. Once again Daniel's refusal to show fear disarmed the Indians, who soon were sitting around the campfire eating venison and laughing and talking with the Boone brothers.

As the night wore on, the Indians produced some cheap French rifles and asked to swap them for Daniel and Squire's more accurate Pennsylvania long rifles. When Daniel refused, the demeanor of the Indians suddenly changed. The Indians quickly overpowered Daniel and Squire and stole not only their rifles but also their skins and the horses that carried them. For the second time on his trip to Kentucky, Daniel Boone had been robbed of everything he had.

Since they could do nothing about the situation, Daniel and Squire set out walking. After several days they came to the cabin of a frontier family, who supplied them with new rifles and horses to make the rest of the journey home.

Finally Daniel made it back home to the small community on Beaver Creek in North Carolina. He arrived late in the afternoon, in the middle of a community dance. After two years in the wilderness, his hair and beard were long and disheveled, and no one seemed to recognize him. He stood at the edge of the crowd and watched the people dance. Rebecca was dancing with several men from the community, and Daniel decided to play a trick on her. He stepped up to her, stretched out his hand, and asked her to dance.

A look of shock spread over Rebecca's face at the man's unkempt appearance. Rebecca did not even recognize the man as her husband. "I'm sorry, sir, but I cannot dance with you," she said politely.

"You need not refuse," Daniel said with a smile. "You have danced many times with me."

Suddenly Rebecca recognized her husband. She threw her arms around him and hugged and kissed him. As the two of them danced, Daniel dreamed of taking Rebecca into Kentucky with him. She would be the first white woman to settle in the Kentucky wilderness, if only she would agree to go.

Chapter 8

Massacre

Over the next week Daniel caught up on local events. Many things had happened while he had been away. One of the most significant was the Battle of Alamance River. It had begun when some Regulators had stormed the court, beat up the officials, including the sheriff, and liberated all of the Regulators who had been tried for not paying the proper taxes and fees. This action brought sheriffs from the eastern counties to hunt down the Regulators who were responsible for liberating the prisoners. A bloody confrontation, the Battle of Alamance River, followed, in which six Regulators leaders were hanged. As a result, all citizens of North Carolina were required to take an oath of allegiance to the government and promise to pay any taxes or fees levied on them.

Daniel hated hearing about such things. He had moved to the Beaver Creek area to be in the wilderness and not be bothered by lawyers and politicians arguing over money. Even though his exploration of Kentucky had been exhausting and difficult, news of the conflicts and battles in Beaver Creek convinced Daniel that he and his family would be happier in the Kentucky wilderness. He immediately began planning his return.

By June of 1773, Rebecca had agreed to go along with Daniel's plans. The Boones decided to wait until after the birth of their eighth child and set out for Kentucky in September that year.

While he waited for the arrival of the new baby, Daniel made a hunting trip westward and stopped in to visit Captain William Russell at the settlement of Castle's Wood, on the Clinch River in southwest Virginia. Russell was a captain in the militia and a well-known trader, tobacco farmer, and justice of the peace. When he heard of Daniel's plan to take his family to Kentucky, he became very excited. He, too, longed to head westward, and soon he and Daniel had made plans to take about one hundred people through the mountains to Kentucky.

So much had to be done before they all set out. As far as Daniel was concerned, his family was emigrating permanently, just as his grandfather had emigrated from England to the new land fifty-four years before and his father had set out from Pennsylvania thirty-three years after that. The land that lay farther to the west now beckoned another generation of Boones.

Daniel sold his farm and cabin and most of the equipment and furniture that went with them. There was only a mere buffalo trail trail through the Cumberland Gap, wide enough for only one horse at a time to pass. As a result, Daniel, Rebecca, and their eight children could take only a few items with them. Daniel knew that food for the journey and the seeds they would need to plant crops once they got to Kentucky would take up most of the available space on the packhorses they would use.

Before they left, Daniel and Rebecca and their children traveled sixty miles to the forks of the Yadkin settlement to say good-bye to their families. As Daniel described the land and the opportunities in Kentucky to them, he convinced about forty of Rebecca's Bryan relatives, all men, to join the traveling party. If they liked what they saw in Kentucky, they would return to Yadkin, sell their homesteads, and follow the Boones to Kentucky to help form a permanent settlement there. The Bryan men suggested that they meet up with Daniel and his family at Moccasin Gap, since it seemed a waste of time and energy to travel to Beaver Creek before setting out for Kentucky.

During the visit Daniel was not able to convince any more of his side of the family to join the new venture, though his brother Squire had already agreed to join him for the journey. While in Yadkin Daniel had to say good-bye to his aging mother. He felt sure he would never see her again, and the two of them wept as they bid each other farewell.

With heavy hearts Daniel and Rebecca returned to Beaver Creek to begin the long journey west to Kentucky. Each packhorse they took had a buffalo rug under its cargo. At night the rugs were used for bedding. The Boone family carried few household items with them, just a butter churn, some twenty-gallon kettles, and a flour sifter—the necessities for setting up a home in the wilderness. Cattle and hogs were driven along, while chickens with their legs tied were carried on one of the packhorses.

Baby Jesse, three-year-old Rebecca, and little Daniel Morgan all traveled in woven hickory baskets strapped to the horses, while the five older children—Levina, Jemima, Susannah, Israel, and the oldest son, sixteen-year-old James—walked alongside their parents. (Daniel's two nephews, Jonathan and Jesse, decided to stay in North Carolina, as Jesse was married and Jonathan was courting a girl.)

In mid-August Daniel and his family met up with the Bryan men at Moccasin Gap, and together they traveled on to Captain Russell's farm on the Clinch River. When it was time to leave there, Captain Russell and his co-traveler, David Gass, were not quite ready to join the rest of the group. They still had several things to take care of and promised that they would catch up with the rest of the group within a few days. So the group set out without them.

As Daniel led the group through the mountains, he began to realize that he had underestimated just how slowly they would travel with so many women and small children. Fearing they would run out of supplies before they reached their destination, he sent his son James and two brothers, John and Richard Mendenhall, back to ask Captain Russell to get more supplies for the journey. The trail back was easy to follow, and Daniel was not worried about their safety.

A week later, on the morning of October 10, 1773, when everyone was gathered around the campfire for breakfast, someone noticed that Tom Hall, one of the other boys in the party, was not there. Tom had been trouble from the start of the journey, pilfering food and refusing to carry his assigned load. Now he and a horse were missing.

Daniel had only a few minutes to ponder the situation before he heard the sound of galloping hooves. He turned to see Tom riding full-speed into camp. Tom climbed off his horse and vomited on the ground. Several people gathered around him.

"What's wrong?" Daniel asked, seeing the fear in Tom's eyes.

Tom wiped his mouth and stuttered. "I ran off...and I'm sorry...and...but...you don't know what I seen." He turned to Daniel. "There was six or seven of them, and I think one of them was James, but I didn't hang about to get a proper look."

Daniel froze. "Tell us, boy, what happened?"

"There was blood and dead bodies everywhere."

"Where?" Daniel asked.

"Over at the ford we passed by a while back. What did you call it? Walden's Creek?"

"Were there any signs of Indians?" Daniel asked.

"Don't know who else could have done it. I couldn't look for long, though," Tom said, vomiting again.

By now everyone in camp was gathered around Tom as the men discussed what to do. If Indians were on the warpath, then the first thing they had to do was protect themselves. Daniel knew he needed to stay with the group and post lookouts, so Squire and several of the other men volunteered to head back to Walden's Creek to bury the dead and search for survivors.

Once this was decided, Daniel ordered everyone capable to do so to pick up a rifle and prepare to defend themselves. As he spoke, he saw Rebecca out of the corner of his eye pull something from one of the saddlebags. It was a white linen sheet. He watched her as she walked over to Squire and handed the sheet to him just before he rode away. Daniel's shoulders slumped as he realized she meant it as a funeral shroud for their son. Still, Daniel hoped that James had managed to escape the massacre. James had been hunting with Daniel since he was seven years old, and Daniel told himself that if anyone could disappear into the woods, it would be James.

It was an agonizing wait for news. The minutes and hours dragged on as Daniel and those waiting behind in the camp listened for one of two sounds: the galloping of horses bringing news of the boys and men or the crackling of twigs and the swoosh of leaves as a war party of Indians crept up on them.

Finally the sound of horses' hooves was heard, and Squire galloped into view, along with Captain Russell and David Gass. Daniel could tell from the look on his brother's face that he was bringing bad news.

Four people were dead at Walden's Creek: the Mendenhall brothers, James Boone, and Henry Russell. Captain Russell had sent his seventeen-year-old son, Henry, woodsman Isaac Crabtree, another youth named Michael Drake, and two slaves, Charles and Adam, on ahead with James Boone and the Mendenhall brothers while he and David followed a day later. William and David had happened upon the scene of the massacre just as Squire and his party arrived. The others—Isaac, Michael, Charles, and Adam—were nowhere to be found.

Daniel asked how his son had died, and Squire told him he had been shot in both hips and then tortured. Squire told Daniel how he had wrapped James and Henry together in one sheet and the Mendenhall brothers in another and buried all four of them in a common grave. James's suffering was almost too much for Daniel to imagine, and he asked Squire to spare Rebecca the details of their son's death.

The dreadful news divided the party. Daniel and some of the other men wanted to press on toward Kentucky, but the majority of the group were eager to turn back. Some even said they would go back alone if they had to. Daniel admitted that it was hopeless to go on, that a fractured party would not travel safely or properly. With great sadness, he ordered them all to turn around for the forty-mile trek back to Castle's Wood. As they retraced their steps, the party somberly walked past Walden's Creek and the communal grave of the four boys.

When they reached Castle's Wood, Adam the slave and Isaac Crabtree were already there. They told a chilling story of escape. Early in the morning, a party of fifteen Delaware, two Cherokee, and two Shawnee had surprised the sleeping group. They opened fire, killing John and Richard Mendenhall instantly. Isaac sprinted off into the woods, while Adam rolled under a nearby log. From that hiding place Adam witnessed James and Henry being shot in the hips and then tortured. Charles, the other slave, was taken prisoner. Neither Adam nor Isaac knew what had happened to Michael Drake.

The eyewitness accounts spurred most of the travelers on. The Bryan men set off for Yadkin the following day, while Squire led the rest of the group back to Beaver Creek. Daniel could not bring himself to return with them. To his way of thinking, there was nothing to go back to. He had sold everything he owned there and staked his hopes on opening up Kentucky. Now he had lost both his oldest son and his dreams. When David Gass offered the Boones the use of a cabin at Castle's Wood for the winter, Daniel accepted the offer. The Boones moved in with their few meager belongings, and Daniel took up his rifle and went off to shoot game. It was the only way he knew to sustain his family through the long winter months.

Every now and then Daniel heard some fresh rumor about the aftermath of the massacre at Walden's Creek. Hunters found the body of the second slave, Charles, about forty miles from the scene. Charles had been murdered with a hatchet. In the spring, Isaac Crabtree attacked three innocent Cherokees enjoying themselves at a horserace. He had killed one Cherokee before the crowd could drag him away. A reward was posted for Crabtree's arrest, but it was doubtful any white settler would turn him in.

Other settlers who had nothing to do with the massacre took out their hatred on Indians as well. On the Ohio River, a group of white men lured a number of Mingo Indians into their camp. They got them drunk and then killed and scalped them all, including a pregnant woman. The Mingos then swore they would kill every settler who crossed their path.

William Russell, whose son Henry was buried with James Boone, also swore vengeance, promising to spend the rest of his life hunting down Indians.

The constant, bloody fighting saddened Daniel a great deal. He thought back to his childhood in Pennsylvania, where the Indians and the Quakers had lived in peace together. How far away that all seemed to him now.

Still, the push westward went on. As soon as the ice on the Ohio River began to crack, surveying parties, most of them financed by wealthy men like

Governor Dunmore of Virginia, headed over the Appalachian Mountains ready to stake out Kentucky. As Daniel watched the surveying teams pass through the Clinch River Valley, he longed to go with them, but he needed to continue hunting to buy food for his family.

He also had promised to help find the body of his friend James Green, who had died on a hunting trip during the winter, and give him a proper burial. James had gone hunting with his brother-in-law far into the mountains. According to the brother-in-law, a bear had attacked James and mauled him to death. The brother-in-law had left James's body in the small bivouac they had built and fled back to Castle's Wood. Now he was leading Daniel and several other men to the site of their hunting camp so that they could give James a proper burial.

The men were several days into the journey and climbing into the mountains when to their utter amazement they met James hobbling down the mountain. His right eye was missing, and that side of his face had been mauled to shreds by the bear, as had his legs and arms. A tale of treachery soon unfolded. On the pretext of going to hunt game for them to eat, James's brother-in-law had abandoned James to die following the bear attack. But James had managed to beat the odds. He had gouged out a hole in the ground and crawled into it, covering himself with wild turkey feathers for warmth. Through the winter he had survived on snow and the bear jerky the two men had taken with them. With the arrival of spring, James had made himself a crutch so that he could hobble down the mountain to safety.

Daniel was enraged by such inhumanity. By leaving James to die, the brother-in-law had acted just as savagely as the Indians who had attacked Daniel's son James and the other boys. Daniel hoped that he never had the misfortune to have such a merciless man with him on any of his hunting and exploring trips.

Chapter 9

"There Is a Dark Cloud Over That Country"

By May 1774 the western mountains and the plains beyond them were in an uproar. Pioneers, trappers, surveyors, and Indians were locked in an endless cycle of killing. Regrettably, this was exactly what Governor Dunmore of Virginia appeared to want. It suited his political purposes to stir up strife so that he could declare an all-out war on the Indians and drive them out of their homelands for good.

In June the same year, Daniel was asked to ride into Kentucky to warn the many Virginia surveyors who were already dividing the land that "Lord Dunmore's War" had begun and that they needed to flee to safety. This was just the type of assignment Daniel loved. He chose a German man named Michael Stoner to be his companion. Daniel had only one day to get ready and say goodbye to his family, and then they were off.

The pair traveled eight hundred miles in sixty-one days. Daniel and Michael found evidence that surveyors had been in the area, but were not able to find any of them. It was not until they arrived back at Castle's Wood in the Clinch River Valley in late August that they learned that a surveyor had been killed in an Indian attack while the rest had straggled into the border settlements.

More bad news awaited Daniel. Shawnee warriors had attacked and killed a number of settlers north of Castle's Wood. This had caused general panic in all of the settlements in the Clinch River Valley, and several small forts had been built while Daniel was away. His own family stayed in Moore's Fort, located a few miles south of the cabin where the Boone family had stayed. But there were few men to man the forts. The governor had called for militiamen to fight the Indians farther north, where they were a bigger threat, promising them that they could keep the Indian horses they stole as a reward. All but a handful of men took up the challenge and galloped off, leaving the women and children with minimal protection. When Daniel returned, Rebecca told him an alarming yet amusing story that demonstrated just how minimal that protection was.

"The men and boys left behind are lazy," she said. "They hardly took our safety seriously. The first time we were forted, they didn't even secure the gate before they went out to play ball. Some of them even lay in the afternoon sun outside the fort without their guns. I wish you had been here, but since you weren't, Susannah, Jemima, and I, along with two of the other women, decided to do something about it."

"What did you do?" Daniel asked.

"We loaded half a dozen guns—not too heavily—and we crept out of the back entrance to the fort, hid in the bushes, and fired into the air. Then we ran back into the fort and slammed the gates shut before the men knew what had happened. You should have seen them, Daniel," Rebecca said with shining eyes. "We climbed up on the parapet just in time to see the men dash for the gate. When they found it was bolted, they didn't know what to do. Some of them dived into bushes, while others jumped into the duck pond and hid themselves in the rushes. After ten minutes we shouted out what we had done and how it proved that they were not ready to defend the fort."

"What happened next?" Daniel asked. "I don't suppose the men were too impressed with your ruse."

Rebecca nodded. "They certainly weren't. When we let them back in, some of them threatened to whip us, and several fights broke out as others tried to stop them. In the end no one was hurt, and the men got a whole lot more serious about our safety."

As it turned out, William Russell was also worried about the safety of the people living in the Clinch River Valley, and he assigned Daniel to lead a troop of fourteen rangers to patrol the forts in the valley and bring discipline and order to them. During the time that the Boone family had lived in Castle's Wood, they had earned a great deal of trust. Still, it was a surprise to Daniel when the settlers circulated a petition asking that he be given the rank of captain and put in charge of all of their safety.

Daniel Boone and his rangers were not at Fort Blackmore on September 23, 1774, when the first attack in the valley occurred. A Mingo Indian chief named John Logan commanded the attack. His mother was an Indian and his father a Frenchman who had been captured by the Oneida tribe years before and later adopted by them. It was John Logan's pregnant sister who had been mercilessly killed and scalped by the group of white men near the Ohio River ten months earlier.

The Indian raiders killed all of the livestock grazing outside Fort Blackmore and captured two black slaves. The following evening Chief Logan and his warriors surprised the Roberts family, who lived thirty miles south of Blackmore's Ford. John Roberts was a forester and had not "forted up" with the others. He, along with his wife and four of his children, was tomahawked to death. A ten-year-old boy managed to get away and was the only member of the family to survive the attack.

When help arrived, they found that Chief Logan had left a note on the body of one of his victims. A white hostage the chief was holding had written down the message, which read:

> Why did you kill my people on Yellow Creek? The white people killed my kin in Conestoga, a great while ago, on Yellow Creek, and took my cousin prisoner. Then I thought I must kill too: And have been three times to war since. But the Indians are not angry, only myself.
>
> Chief John Logan

A week later the chief and his band struck at Moore's Fort. As sunset approached, after checking that all was clear around the fort, three men left the fort to check a pigeon trap set about three hundred yards from the stockade. Before the men reached the trap, gunfire erupted from the surrounding bush. One of the men fell dead immediately, while the other two managed to dive for cover in nearby bushes. When the men in the fort heard the gunfire, they came rushing out, but by then the Indians had fled, taking with them the scalp of the man they had just shot.

The next incident occurred when Chief Logan targeted Fort Blackmore for a second time. This time, however, the settlers were more ready for him, and the only person killed during the raid was a young guard who did not get back inside the gate of the fort fast enough. He was stranded outside the stockade and was shot.

Although there were no more attacks on the forts in the Clinch River Valley, Lord Dunmore's War went on until October 10, 1774, when, at Point Pleasant on the Ohio River, an army of one thousand Virginia soldiers surrounded a group of three hundred Shawnee and Delaware Indians and opened fire. In the fighting eighty soldiers were killed and another one hundred fifty were wounded. Despite their losses, the soldiers managed to march to and surround the Shawnee towns on the Scioto River. The Shawnee finally surrendered and agreed to sign treaties giving the colonial governments the rights to settle their lands. In what became known as the Treaty of Camp Charlotte, the Shawnee chiefs agreed to cede their hunting grounds in Kentucky for Lord Dunmore's promise that all settlers into the area would be kept south of the Ohio River.

Not long after the Treaty of Camp Charlotte was signed, a North Carolina lawyer, Richard Henderson, entered into negotiations of his own with the Cherokee tribe to purchase twenty million acres of their hunting grounds in Kentucky. The chief of the tribe tentatively agreed to the deal, in which Henderson would give them approximately fifty thousand dollars worth of goods. A large meeting of the tribe was scheduled for March 1775, when the agreement would finally be ratified.

In the meantime, Henderson asked Daniel if he would take on the monumental task of marking out the best passage for a road that would take settlers from Virginia through the Cumberland Gap and into Kentucky and then, selecting a good spot, found a town there. Daniel was delighted with the challenge and even more pleased with the reward for completing the task: his choice of two thousand acres of the land Henderson held title to in Kentucky.

Daniel could hardly wait to get to work. He was convinced that this emigration would be easier and more efficient than the attempt two years earlier that had ended in the death of his son James. For one thing, many Indian tribes had since entered into peaceful agreements with white settlers. And this time an armed troop of woodsmen would go ahead of the women and children to cut a wide swath through the wilderness so that the whole group would not have to walk single file.

With these new conditions and the generous pay of ten pounds apiece, Daniel had no difficulty recruiting thirty relatives and neighbors to build the new road. One of these men was a twenty-year-old Irishman named William Hays. William took a liking to fourteen-year-old Susannah Boone, and the two of them were married before the expedition set out. Susannah, the new bride, signed on to cook for the thirty men. A slave woman who belonged to one of the other men on the expedition served as her assistant.

In early March 1775, Daniel watched as over a thousand Cherokee men, women, and children gathered at Sycamore Shoals on the south side of the Watauga River, where they talked and debated among themselves the sale of their hunting grounds to Henderson. The members of the tribe expressed some opposition to the sale. Several men pointed out that this was land that not only they but also other tribes hunted on, and they doubted that the tribe could sell it. Eventually a consensus to sell the land was agreed upon among the tribe, and a deed was drawn up passing the land to

Richard Henderson and the Transylvania Company he had founded to oversee the settlement of it.

During the proceedings, Dragging Canoe, a young Cherokee chief, looked west and remarked, “There is a dark cloud over that country.” The Cherokee’s caution was made even more ominous when the negotiations were finally completed. Chief Oconostota, one of the main Cherokee chiefs, turned to Daniel and took hold of his hand. “Brother,” the chief said, “we have given you a fine land, but I believe you will have much trouble in settling it.”

Chapter 10

The Wilderness Road

The work crew who would build what was being called the Wilderness Road met on the Virginia-Tennessee border. Daniel arrived with his brother Squire, daughter Susannah, and her husband, William. The plan was to follow as much as possible the contours of the Warrior's Trail that led to Kentucky, clearing and widening the path.

The first tree on the project was felled on March 10, 1775, and Daniel estimated it would take a month to complete the project. He planned to be back at Castle's Wood in Virginia in three months, in time for the birth of their ninth child. Daniel hoped the child's arrival would ease some of the pain Rebecca still felt over the death of James.

Life building the Wilderness Road soon fell into a pattern. Daniel was the first up in the morning. He helped Susannah rekindle the fire and ate some breakfast with her before riding out ahead of the workers to mark the trail. When he had done this, he would veer off into the woods, hunting for wild game to bring back for everyone's supper. In the meantime the men had set to work hacking at the uneven rock path with pickaxes, chopping down trees, and clearing brush. While the men worked, Susannah and her assistant packed up the camp and transported it to the new trailhead, where they began cooking dinner for the men.

The spring thaw was late that year, and the men were frequently caught in snowstorms or freezing rain. The exhausting work of clearing and widening the path was tested when the team reached the pass at Cumberland Gap. Because the pass was flanked on both sides by high mountains of solid stone, it was difficult for the men to make the existing trail wide enough for packhorses to pass through. Still, they pressed on.

Three backbreaking weeks after they started, the crew hacked their way into Kentucky. It was a triumphant moment as Daniel looked out over the land that he had fought so hard to make a way for others to enter. Susannah Boone Hays and her slave assistant were the first non-Indian women to enter Kentucky.

The crew pitched camp beside a spring and slept soundly until half an hour before sunrise, when the sound of warriors running into camp woke everyone up in an instant of fear. Daniel reached for his gun and fired upon the invaders, as did several of the other men, but not before the invaders had killed one of the road builders named Twitty, his slave Sam, and Twitty's bulldog. Another man named Walker was seriously injured in the attack. Thankfully, the rest of the group were able to flee into the surrounding trees and survived. When the attack was over, several men packed up their belongings and headed back to civilization through the Cumberland Gap.

Daniel was concerned about the attack, too, but for a different reason. He feared that news of the Indian raid would discourage other pioneers from setting out for Kentucky. And he hoped that the group Richard Henderson was already leading along the newly cut Wilderness Road did not turn back. He wrote a letter to Henderson that he started off by outlining the tragic events of the Indian attack. Then he wrote:

> My advice to you Sir, is to come or send as soon as possible. Your company is desired greatly, for the people are very uneasy but are willing to stay and venture their lives with you, and now is the time to flusterate the intentions of the Indians, and keep the country whilst we are in it. If we give way to them now, it will ever be the case. This day we start from the battle ground, for the mouth of Otter Creek, where we shall immediately erect a fort, which will

> be done before you can come or send—then we can send ten men to meet you, if you send for them.

Daniel signed and dispatched the letter, giving the messenger instructions to go as quickly as he could while watching out for Indians. The last thing they needed now was another bloody encounter.

On April 2, 1775, one of the woodsmen called Daniel over to where he was working. "Look at this," he said. "Any telling how old it is?"

Daniel peered into the hollow of a sycamore tree. A human skeleton was wedged inside. Daniel removed it one bone at a time. Near the bottom of the pile lay a powder horn, on which were carved the initials "J.S." Daniel stared at the horn for a long time. It was his brother-in-law John Stuart's horn. Daniel recalled the day he had gone searching for John and how he had found an abandoned fire but no sign of him. Now Daniel guessed that John had been attacked by Indians and, wounded, sought refuge in the hollow of the tree, where he had bled to death.

That evening Daniel dug a grave, and together with the other men, held a short service before burying John's bones. At least, when he next saw his sister Hannah next, he would be able to tell her that her husband had had a proper burial.

On April 6 the road-cutting group reached their destination, a sloping flood plain on the south bank of the Kentucky River a short distance downstream from the mouth of Otter Creek. Across the fast-flowing river, the heavily wooded bank rose steeply, secluding and protecting the site. Two springs bubbled up nearby, one with fresh water, enough to supply the community they planned to establish there, and the other with brackish water that left the surrounding ground salt-laden. This salt lick attracted many animals, who came to drink and lick the salty ground. All this animal activity over the years had made the soil of the flood plain rich and fertile for growing crops.

Thoughts of Indian attack after they had arrived at the site spurred the men on to cut logs and construct a makeshift twelve-foot high stockade. The men named their shelter Fort Boone and posted a round-the-clock sentinel above the gate.

On April 20, Richard Henderson and his party of settlers arrived at Fort Boone. When Daniel spied them in the distance, he ordered his men to fire a welcoming volley. In such a hostile land, it was a great relief to get reinforcements, and Richard and Daniel gave each other a hearty handshake.

"Seeing that you are still here has dropped a load off my shoulders," Richard said. "It is only because of the confidence the men have in you that we have gotten this far. Let's hope we can go on together and build a strong settlement."

A few days later, Richard proposed that the settlement's name be changed from Fort Boone to Boonesborough. Once that was agreed upon, the eighty white men present drew lots for two-acre plots of land around the settlement where they could plant corn and other crops for the summer. The men were also granted much more land farther afield in the Kentucky wilderness.

Almost immediately the bickering started. Men were not pleased with their portions of land. Not only this, the other two hundred white men in Kentucky, most of them from the settlement of Harrodsburg, were disputing the Transylvania Company's right to the land around Boonesborough.

In an attempt to smooth over the situation, Richard Henderson called for a convention. Daniel and Squire Boone and two other men were elected to represent Boonesborough. When the delegates from Harrodsburg arrived, they all met together under a huge elm tree near where the men had begun to build a larger, stronger stockade.

The delegates discussed many issues of concern to the two communities and smoothed out many of their differences. They then passed a bill that created a court system that would punish criminals and order debt collection, and a bill for the establishment of a militia.

One of Daniel's main concerns was the preservation of the wildlife. He had seen that the men could not resist the urge to hunt and kill buffalo. Much to his dismay, many of them did so for sport, just so they could brag about how many buffalo they had shot. They would cut off the hump or the tongue of the animal and leave the rest of the carcass to rot where it had fallen. Not surprisingly, buffalo herds soon became scarce around Boonesborough. Within a month of their arrival, the men had to ride fifteen or twenty miles to find one. Daniel proposed that restrictions be put on hunting so that an animal's entire carcass had to be used by the man who killed the animal. He also wanted incentives for those men who bred horses, as Daniel was sure that an ample supply of horses was a key to a strong settlement.

Just as the convention was ending, a messenger arrived with startling news. The battles of Lexington and Concord had occurred on April 19. The colonists were rising up against their British rulers!

Daniel's mind was occupied with more immediate, practical matters. By June, Boonesborough had run out of salt, which was needed to jerk meat and preserve vegetables. Most of the salt that had been intended for the new settlement had been left on the other side of the Cumberland Gap when they had unloaded there. Daniel headed back to the Clinch River Valley to bring back a new supply of salt after first going home to see whether Rebecca had given birth to their new baby.

Sadly, Rebecca's pregnancy had been a difficult one, and within days of Daniel's return, Rebecca bore a small and sickly son, whom they named William. William lived only a few days. Instead of easing the sorrow at the loss of their firstborn son, this new baby's short life and sudden death only added to Rebecca and Daniel's heartache.

Daniel was still convinced that the best thing for his family would be to move to Kentucky. As soon as Rebecca was well enough, they set out. Daniel had also rounded up seventeen young men who were willing to go along, as well as three other families. All in all, fifty people loaded their goods onto packhorses and headed out of the valley in mid-August. Once they had passed through the Cumberland Gap, half of the group, including the other three families, took the left fork that led to Harrodsburg.

It was a joyous moment when the Boone family and the single young men reached Boonesborough. Daniel smiled as Rebecca and the children were reunited with Susannah, who was pregnant by now.

Life at the settlement had become even more uneasy. Many men felt that their job was finished once the Wilderness Road was complete. Despite the threat of Indian attack, many of the men refused to guard the main camp. It seemed that once they had obtained their own plot of land, they were reluctant to pitch in and help construct the two-story permanent stockade that Richard Henderson had planned on. The longer the stockade remained unfinished, the more vulnerable the settlement became to Indian invasion and attack.

The families of the settlement were also having financial problems. In September the directors of the Transylvania Company doubled what they charged settlers for land, yet they sold land very cheaply to big landholders back East. They also announced that the taxes on the land would double to two shillings per hundred acres. Many of the settlers had no money to pay the taxes, since they relied on farming and hunting for their sustenance.

At the same time, Richard Henderson traveled to the Virginia Convention to request a claim to Kentucky for the Transylvania Company. Two delegates representing settlers opposed to Henderson's group also attended the convention and presented a petition requesting that Kentucky be part of Virginia. The outcome was in the settlers' favor. Instead of voting to recognize the Transylvania Company's land as a separate province, the convention resolved that the Kentucky settlers should hold their lands.

The Virginia Convention had taken notice of the things the Transylvania Company was doing. Thomas Jefferson argued that the outfit was operating more like a kingdom than a company. Daniel soon learned that the convention had invalidated all of the Transylvania Company's land claims and, with them, Henderson's grant of two thousand acres to him. Some of the settlers decided to sue Henderson.

Although he would never receive the title to the land Richard Henderson had promised him, Daniel did not sue. He had come to understand that living on the frontier meant taking serious risks. The time was approaching, though, when Daniel would have to risk much more than just a land claim.

Chapter 11

Kidnapped

It was Sunday afternoon July 14, 1776, and Daniel Boone was sound asleep, taking an afternoon nap in the log cabin he had built for his family. He was awakened from his sleep by the commotion going on in the village, and then he heard someone screaming, "The savages have taken the girls."

On hearing this, Daniel leaped out of bed, grabbed his rifle, and bolted from the cabin. He was still dressed in his woolen Sunday trousers, and his feet were bare.

Outside Daniel learned the grim news. A band of Indians had taken three Boonesborough girls captive—his fourteen-year-old daughter Jemima and the Callaway sisters, Betsy and Frances. The girls had apparently been canoeing on the river and ventured too close to the other side, where they were grabbed by the Indians. Nobody had actually seen the girls being captured. People in the vicinity had just heard their screams, and the canoe was now lying swamped on the far side of the river about a quarter of a mile downstream from Boonesborough. Immediately Daniel ran to the spot opposite the canoe.

Daniel reached the spot just as a group of men on horseback rode up behind him. The riders quickly agreed that they should gallop the mile downstream to the ford and cross the river there and then loop back to see if they could find the Indians' trail. In the meantime John Gass, one of the young boys of the community, dived into the river and swam to the other side. Daniel and several of the other men kept their rifles at the ready in case Indians attacked John as he bailed the water out of the canoe and paddled back across the river. As soon as John reached shore, Daniel and four of the men jumped into the canoe with John and paddled back to the other side. They clambered up the steep bluff that rose from the river and began looking for the Indians' trail. They had no sooner found it than the men on horseback rode up.

From the direction of the tracks, Daniel knew that the Indians would be heading north to the Indian communities in the Ohio country. He directed the horsemen to ride to the ford of the Licking River and try to head the Indians off. In the meantime he and the other men would follow the

Indians' trail. Daniel was concerned that if the horses stayed with them, the Indians might kill the girls when they heard the sound of thundering horses' hooves behind them.

Daniel and the others stealthily followed tracks the Indians had left. Then, just as the last rays of the sun were disappearing, they heard a sound a short distance from the left side of the trail. Immediately the men fanned out and began to close in. But instead of finding Indians and the kidnapped girls, they came upon five men building a log cabin.

By now it was completely dark, and Daniel decided they should camp for the night beside the partially built cabin and renew their pursuit at first light. However, neither Daniel nor the men with him were equipped to continue the chase. Daniel was still in his bare feet and wearing his Sunday pants, and the other men had no food with them. Daniel sent twelve-year-old John Gass back to Boonesborough to fetch his deerskin leggings and moccasins and bring back a supply of deer jerky for them to eat.

Before dawn John arrived back in camp with all the supplies requested. Daniel clapped John on the back and commended him for the way he had been able to find his way to Boonesborough and back in the dark. He watched as a big smile of satisfaction settled across John's face.

After eating some jerky and putting on the clothes that John brought back from Boonesborough, the men were ready to begin the chase again. Three of the men building the cabin joined them.

Daniel led the way. Sometimes the tracks went in several directions, as the Indians had split up and then come back together farther ahead. Sometimes the tracks disappeared into a stream, where the Indians walked for several miles in the streambed. The men knew they were on the right trail because along the way they found broken twigs and branches.

"It has to be the girls. They're alive and leaving us a trail to follow," Daniel said with both relief and pride. This knowledge spurred the men on.

Despite the girls' best efforts to mark the way, the Indians' tricks were slowing the men down in their pursuit. Daniel began to grow frustrated as the day wore on.

"This will never do," he finally declared. "The Indians are making tracks faster than we are. From the direction of these tracks, they can be headed for only one place, the crossing of the Licking River where the Upper Blue Lick spring joins it. I know the way there. Follow me!"

With that Daniel veered off the trail and set out through the woods directly for the Licking River crossing. The men followed silently in single file. Now they were making faster time, and after several hours of trotting, they came upon a trail where Daniel once again spotted the Indians' tracks. Soon the men began to notice more broken twigs and even small pieces of ripped fabric that must have come from the girls' dresses.

The men followed the trail until darkness engulfed them, and they made camp for the night. After eating jerky and taking a long drink from a nearby spring, Daniel lay down on the hard earth and went to sleep, his rifle close by at the ready.

The following morning at first light, the men were on the trail once again. Daniel set a cracking pace as he raced after his daughter. He knew they must be starting to catch up with the Indians, and this was confirmed when they came to a stream. The water there was still muddy from the Indians crossing it, and a little farther on, they found a snake one of the Indians had killed. Then, farther along they came upon a butchered buffalo calf. The animal's hump had been cut off, and warm blood still oozed from it.

"We are close," Daniel said. "They obviously think we are a long way behind or have given up the pursuit, and they will stop soon and cook the buffalo meat they have taken with them."

The men had gone only a short distance when Daniel noticed smoke rising. He signaled for the men to stop, and they quickly hatched a rescue plan. Daniel would creep up on the Indians while the others stayed hidden among the trees. No one was to fire a shot until Daniel gave the signal.

The men crept quietly up a small rise and at the top looked down into a dell where the Indians had stopped to cook the buffalo meat. One warrior sat beside the fire slowly turning the meat on a stick over the flames. Another Indian was lighting his pipe in the fire, and still another was lying on his back in the grass. Daniel recognized him as a Cherokee chief named Hanging Maw, whom he'd had dealings with back in North Carolina. Two other Indians were busily gathering wood for the fire. Daniel spotted the girls on the far side of the dell, sitting under an oak tree. The two younger ones sat resting their heads on sixteen-year-old Betsy's lap.

Daniel dropped to the ground and began to crawl on his belly down the rise toward the Indian camp. He was nearly to the bottom when the weight of his hand snapped a twig. Immediately the Indians beside the fire looked up. Daniel pulled himself down as low as he could. When they seemed convinced that the sound had come from a bird or some small animal, the Indians diverted their attention back to what they were doing. Jemima Boone, however, kept scouring the woods. When Daniel finally raised his head again, his eyes met Jemima's. Quickly he raised his hand to his mouth to signal her to be quiet. Just then a shot rang out. One of the men had fired before Daniel gave the signal.

The gunshot hit the Indian tending the meat roasting over the fire, and he fell forward into the flames. He screamed in pain and jumped up, grabbed his belly, and fled into the woods. At the same time more shots rang out. One shot hit Hanging Maw in the hand, and the chief dropped his rifle and fled. The other Indians fled, too, but not before one of them hurled his tomahawk at the girls, narrowly missing Betsy's head. "It's my father; they've come," Jemima shouted as the three girls dived to the ground for cover.

By now the men were charging down the rise and into the camp. Betsy stood up to run toward her rescuers. Because of her dark, disheveled hair, around which was tied an Indian bandanna, one of the men mistook her for a Indian woman running to attack and raised the stock of his rifle to club her. Daniel raced to him and grabbed the man's arm just as he was about to pound the rifle into Betsy's head. "For goodness sake, man, don't kill her when we've traveled so far to save her."

At the sight of her father, Jemima jumped up and ran to meet him. Tears of relief and joy replaced the tears of fear streaming down her face.

Quickly the men and the girls took cover in case the Indians fired at them from the trees. But as Daniel looked around the camp, he realized that they would not fight back. The Indians had fled, leaving their guns and tomahawks, and two of them had even left their moccasins behind. When Daniel pointed this out, everyone breathed a sigh of relief and gathered around the fire. All of the men were overcome by the joy of seeing the girls alive, and soon there was not a dry eye among the entire group.

Finally, after they had all regained their composure, Jemima told her father that Hanging Maw had told her that a raiding party of Indians was holed up at the crossing of the Licking River ready to sweep down and raid white farms and communities in Kentucky. Armed with this information,

Daniel decided they should set out for Boonesborough as quickly as possible. He knew he had taken a huge risk leaving just a few men to defend the place while the others hunted for the captured girls. Still, before they set out, they feasted on the buffalo meat roasting over the fire.

As they ate, the details of the girls' capture came spilling out. Jemima explained that she'd had a sore foot from a stab from a cane frond, and on the Sunday afternoon of the capture, she had thought that dipping it in the cool water of the Kentucky River would help it heal. She had invited Frances and Betsy Callaway to go on a short canoe ride with her. Jemima went on to tell how she was dangling her foot in the water over the side of the canoe while Betsy and Frances paddled when they got caught in the swift current that sent them into an eddy. The eddy eventually spat them out when they were just a few feet from the far side of the river.

"I'm sorry, Father," Jemima said as the story unfolded. "I know you warned us never to cross the river, but we couldn't help it. No matter how hard we tried, we just couldn't battle the current."

Jemima continued to explain that as the girls tried to get control of the canoe, an Indian had leaped out from the riverbank, grabbed the buffalo-hide tug used to tie up the vessel, and pulled the canoe ashore, where the other Indians grabbed the girls.

"We screamed and screamed," Betsy said, "but they threatened us with their tomahawks if we did not stop. We were frightened as they dragged us up the bank and then headed north. We tried to slow them down. We kept deliberately falling over, and every so often we would break a twig or a branch in the hope you would find our trail."

"We did indeed," Daniel said. "That was a very smart thing to do."

"More than once Hanging Maw threatened to kill us when he discovered us doing it, but we kept doing it anyway," Frances interjected.

"But after two days we were starting to lose hope. We were soon going to cross the Licking and head into the Ohio country, where you might not ever find us. And then I looked up and there you were," Jemima said. "I knew you would come. I just knew it." She reached out and hugged her father again.

Soon the group was back on the trail headed to Boonesborough. By the second day the girls were tired; they had slept and eaten little while with the Indians. When a scrawny horse, probably escaped from some hunting party, appeared beside the trail, one of the men caught it. The girls laughed out loud when they saw it.

"It's the same horse the Indians caught," Jemima said. "They tried to make us ride it so they could travel faster, but we pretended we didn't know how to ride and kept falling off. And sometimes we kicked it in the side, and it would rear up and bite at us and throw us to the ground. Finally the Indians got so frustrated they let the animal go, and we kept walking, as slowly as we could, of course, and we kept falling down."

This time, though, the exhausted girls gladly took turns riding on the horse's back, which helped the group make good time on their return to Boonesborough. Daniel was afraid that the departure of the rescue party had left the settlement too vulnerable. He wanted to get home before anything violent happened—if it hadn't already.

Chapter 12

The Gauntlet

The girls and their rescue party arrived safely in Boonesborough the following day, returning at the same time as the riders who had gone to head off the kidnapping Indians. A joyous welcome awaited everyone. Rebecca ran to Jemima and wrapped her in a huge hug. A great celebration followed during which the story of the kidnapping and the rescue was recounted for all to hear.

Daniel had been right to be concerned, though. Just as he feared, several Indian attacks on Boonesborough had occurred in his absence. No one had been killed, but one of the cabins had been burned to the ground and some of the corn crops scorched. Several families, not able to take the strain of the constant threat of Indian attacks, had hastily left Boonesborough, retreating back through the Cumberland Gap to Virginia.

One good thing did come out of the kidnapping. Now, at last, the remaining twenty-two men of the community became serious about building the walls around their settlement, and they worked day and night until the cabins were secure within them.

In addition to constructing and securing the fort, the men had to harvest the crops, hunt for food, collect water from the nearby spring, and defend the settlement's twelve women, thirty children, and ten slaves. The work was difficult and tiring, and tempers flared as the settlers spent day after day cooped up inside the fort.

Then, in the middle of August, a messenger arrived with a piece of paper carefully wrapped in deerskin. Daniel was the first to read it. The document began: "When in the course of human events, it becomes necessary for one people to dissolve the political bands which have connected them with another..." It was a copy of the Declaration of Independence.

Like the other settlements in the west, Boonesborough was divided on the matter of the colonies fighting for freedom from Great Britain. A few of Rebecca's relatives were firmly against the split, while Daniel did not have a strong opinion either way. He was preoccupied with keeping the settlers safe from the Indians, a much more pressing situation than anything that might be happening in Philadelphia, New York, or Boston.

Even so, the folks at Boonesborough did celebrate the Declaration of Independence that night. After reading the document aloud publicly, they held a bonfire and dance. One of the slaves, whom everyone called Uncle Monk, provided the music for the dance on his fiddle. During the dance, Daniel couldn't help but notice that Jemima was spending a lot of time with Flanders Callaway, one of the young men who had rescued her.

For the most part, Boonesborough remained cut off from the colonies and news of the Revolution. Few settlers ventured into Kentucky, and those who did were kept very busy trying to survive. Because at this time Kentucky was part of Virginia, Daniel wrote many letters begging the Virginia government not to forget the Kentucky settlers and in particular to send them gunpowder, as their supplies were running low.

More Indian attacks took place, but no one was kidnapped or killed again until March 7, 1777. Daniel was sharpening his hunting knife just outside his cabin when he heard gunfire. He grabbed his rifle and ran to the gate. Settlers who had been out on their farm lots preparing to plant their crops rushed terrified through the gates of the stockade. One man with a bloody shoulder was carried in. He told Daniel that his slave had been shot dead and that he had rushed back into the forest after the Indian had fired on them.

Rebecca and Jemima took charge of the wounded man while Daniel organized the other men into a scouting party. Not finding any sign of the Indians, they brought the dead slave back into the fort and buried him.

The following day the men divided themselves into two groups of ten. One group farmed the plots outside the fort while the other ten men guarded them. Although it was dangerous for any of them to be outside the fort, they knew that without an adequate harvest, they would starve before the winter was over.

As they worked, news soon reached them that another group of Indians had attacked some men from Harrodsburg the same day as Boonesborough was attacked. The Harrodsburg men had been gathering a wild plant to make sugar with when they were set upon by the Indians. Four of them were killed, adding to the general panic at both forts.

On April 24 the Indians struck Boonesborough again. When the cows refused to go out to pasture and instead stayed near the gate of the fort, Daniel became wary. He wondered if there might be Indians hiding nearby, and he sent two men out to investigate. The men found nothing and turned to go back to the fort. Suddenly a group of Shawnees emerged from a stand of sycamore trees and began firing their rifles at the two men, who bolted for the gate of the fort seventy yards away. One of the men, Daniel Goodman, was shot in the back. After he collapsed, several Shawnees began to scalp him. Simon Kenton, who was standing by the open gate to the fort, raced forward when he saw what was happening. When a Shawnee brave raised Daniel Goodman's scalp into the air, Simon fell to one knee, aimed his rifle, and killed the Indian. The Indian fell to the ground, and the rest of the Shawnees scattered.

No sooner had Simon fired his shot than Daniel Boone and twelve other men ran up to support him. Michael Stoner, who had accompanied Daniel on his mission to warn the surveyors to flee back to Virginia, walked several paces ahead. He saw a warrior crawling among the bushes and raised his rifle and shot him. Before he could reload, several shots rang out from among the trees. Michael dropped his rifle as one lead ball went right through his wrist and another lodged in his hip. As Daniel and the other men ran to help him, three dozen Shawnees blocked the path behind them. The Indians had been lying in wait among the sycamore trees, and Daniel and the other men had walked right into their trap. To get back to the safety of the fort, they would have to fight their way through the Indians.

"We're trapped. We have to fight, boys," Daniel yelled. "Sell your lives as dear as possible."

Daniel knew that the Indians did not like hand-to-hand fighting, preferring to wait until they had the advantage and then exploit it. Sure enough, as the men charged forward, the Shawnees kept backing up until the men had managed to charge through the middle of the Indian line. As the men bolted for the fort, a hail of bullets rang out from the Shawnees' rifles. One of the shots smashed into Daniel's ankle, sending him crashing to the ground. As he lay there dazed, a Shawnee warrior ran up, straddled Daniel, and raised his tomahawk to finish him off. Before he could, Simon fired his rifle, and the Indian fell dead beside Daniel. Another warrior raced toward Daniel with his knife drawn. Simon bounded forward and struck the

Indian across the side of the head with the stock of his rifle before he could get to Daniel. Simon then dragged Daniel into the fort. A hail of bullets whizzed past his head and crashed into the side of the stockade. Moments later William Bush dragged the wounded Michael Stoner into the fort, and the gates were closed to shut out the Indians, who quickly retreated back into the grove of sycamore trees. In all, one man and most of the cattle were killed, and four men were wounded in the attack. Daniel and Michael were the most seriously injured.

Since there were no doctors in Kentucky, Rebecca and several of the other women in the community nursed the wounded men. They extracted the lead shot ball from Daniel's ankle and applied poultices to the men's wounds.

For the next six weeks, Daniel was an invalid while his shattered right ankle healed. However, Jemima and Flanders had fallen in love, and as soon as Daniel was able to stand again he married them in a double wedding with Frances Callaway and John Holder.

Finally, in August 1777, the government of Virginia sent one hundred militiamen into Kentucky to help control the raids. Half of the men were stationed at Harrodsburg, and the others were at Boonesborough. The militiamen arrived just in time, because the British army had a new plan for fighting the rebels. The redcoats, as the British were called, were making their way into the Ohio Valley and paying Indians to kill settlers.

Lieutenant Governor Hamilton, the British governor based in Detroit, even offered a bounty on white scalps, earning him the nickname "Hair-Buyer."

This outraged Daniel and the other settlers, and they became even more determined to hang onto their little outpost. Then good news arrived in mid-November. The American "rebels" had stopped the British advance from Canada. Kentucky was safe for the moment.

The winter of 1777 proved to be the longest one Daniel could recall. The corn harvest had been poor, and the people had little to eat. No new supplies had arrived from the east, and everyone's clothes grew thin and ripped. Some of the women worked out a way to weave the fibers of wild nettles together with buffalo hair. The result was a strong fabric, but it was very itchy when made into clothes.

Three years before, a number of hogs had been brought to the settlement and allowed to forage freely in the nearby forest. Thankfully, they had thrived, and many of their offspring were hunted that winter. In addition, the women followed the last surviving cattle around to see what they ate and then collected those plants themselves to cook with the wild pork.

The stores of gunpowder and bullets had been built up by the arrival of the Virginia militia, but as they wintered over in Boonesborough, supplies of these items once again began to dwindle. Because of this it was essential that on hunting trips every shot find its target and every bit of a carcass be either eaten or preserved. However, to jerk meat the settlers needed salt, and salt was one thing that everyone was running out of.

The water and soil around Boonesborough did provide a rich supply of natural salt. There were many saltwater springs and large salt licks, or areas of salty soil, and hunters were constantly finding new ones. The two largest saltwater springs nearest to the settlement were known as the Blue Licks, which flowed into the Licking River. The water at the lower Blue Licks spring had a higher salt content, and Daniel made plans to lead a group of men to it to replenish their salt supply. There was always an element of danger in leaving the fort, but Daniel was not too worried. Indians had never attacked them in winter, and snow was thick on the ground.

In January 1778 Daniel and twenty-nine men from both the community and the militia set out from Boonesborough. Several days later they were camped beside the Licking River at the lower Blue Licks spring. They set up huge kettles and began boiling down the springwater. As the water evaporated, they scraped the salt left behind from the sides of the kettles. In this way they could make large quantities of salt in one day.

On the morning of February 7, Daniel and two other men, Flanders Callaway and Thomas Brooks, set out to hunt game for the men to eat. Daniel rode to the southwest while the other two made their way up the Licking River.

It was a freezing cold day. When Daniel spotted a deer ahead, he silently dismounted and stalked the animal. His shot found its mark. Once the animal was dead, Daniel skinned it and cut it up into pieces, which he loaded onto the back of his horse. He had just finished tying the pieces onto his horse when to his surprise he noticed four Shawnee warriors closing in on him. Daniel reached for his knife so that he could cut his horse free and flee, but he had put the knife away with blood still on it, and now it was frozen into its sheath. Daniel fled on foot, running as fast as he could through the snow. The Indians gave chase, and being much younger than Daniel, they began to gain on him. When several bullets crashed into the snow beside him, Daniel realized he could not outrun them. He stopped, walked to a tree, leaned his rifle against it, a sign of surrender, and turned to face the Shawnee warriors. "How d' do," he said to them with a smile, reaching out his hand to shake theirs.

This time, Daniel's friendly attitude did not disarm his attackers, who were intent on taking Daniel with them. Daniel knew he had no choice but to follow. He was marched three miles to where about 120 Shawnee warriors were camped. Two French traders, neither of whom spoke English, were at the camp, as was an ex-slave named Pompey, who acted as a translator for the Shawnee chief Blackfish. Daniel's arrival in camp created quite a stir among the Shawnee, many of whom either had personally fought against Daniel or knew the stories about his encounters with other Indians. Many of the warriors wanted to shake the hand of this legendary adversary.

A short time later Pompey told Daniel that Chief Blackfish wanted to talk to him. As they trudged through the snow to the chief's tent, Daniel set about learning all he could from Pompey. He discovered that the British had sent the two Frenchmen to help the Indians kill settlers. Daniel was astounded to hear why the Shawnees were on the warpath in the dead of winter. Three months before, in November, Shawnee Chief Cornstalk had gone to Point Pleasant, on the Ohio River, to talk to the American commander of the fort there. Cornstalk was well respected as a man of peace, and the Indians were shocked when the Americans at the fort took Cornstalk, his son, and his entourage prisoner. Then a group of frontiersmen overran the prison where they were being held and shot all of the Shawnees, including Chief Cornstalk, in their cells.

It was a bitter blow to the Indians who supported Cornstalk and his peaceful intentions. Young Shawnee warriors called for revenge and joined Chief Blackfish to form a war party. At first they wanted to extract revenge against the fort at Point Pleasant, but it was too well fortified for an easy attack. Instead they set their sights to the south, deciding to attack and destroy Boonesborough. And now they had had a lucky break. Not only had the four warriors captured Daniel Boone, but also they brought news that twenty-seven men from Boonesborough were camped along the Licking River.

Chief Blackfish was a short, wiry man in his late forties who got straight down to business when Daniel arrived. The two men sat facing each other, with Pompey acting as translator.

"Who are the men camped by the salt spring?" Blackfish asked.

"They are my men," Daniel replied courteously.

"We have come to destroy your village on the Kentucky River in revenge for the death of Cornstalk at the hand of the long knives (whites). Before we do, we will go back and kill your men at the spring," Blackfish told Daniel.

Daniel had to think fast. The Shawnees outnumbered the men at the salt lick by nearly four to one. It would be no match. The men from Boonesborough would be easily killed. And if the men were gone, Boonesborough would be easily routed and destroyed. Only the women and children were there, along with a handful of militiamen. They could not hold off an assault on the fort for long.

Quickly Daniel came up with a plan he thought might buy them all some time and eventually spare the lives of his men and the people at Boonesborough. He told Blackfish that the long knives who killed Cornstalk were dishonorable men, not like the people of Boonesborough. However, if attacked, the men at the salt spring would surely fight back, and in the process many Shawnee warriors would die as well. Daniel proposed a compromise. If Daniel convinced his men to surrender peacefully to the Indians, the chief must promise that he would not harm Daniel's men or make any of them run the gauntlet—the Shawnee method of torturing prisoners. Daniel then told the chief that the people at Boonesborough would fight hard rather than be taken prisoner and dragged off in the dead of winter. Then he led Blackfish to believe that if he waited till the spring, the people of the settlement might be more likely to surrender after a harsh winter and a poor corn crop. They would be weary of fighting and would go with the Shawnee to live in their towns in the Ohio country. After a long pause, the chief decided to accept Daniel's terms for the surrender of his men, and he promised he would not attack Boonesborough until spring.

Early the next morning, Daniel and the Shawnees set out for the Blue Licks spring. When they arrived, the men from Boonesborough looked up in astonishment to watch Daniel lead the Indians into their camp. Daniel held his hand up so they would not shoot and then tried to explain the situation to them. It wasn't easy. The men wanted to stand and fight, but eventually Daniel convinced them all to surrender peacefully to the Shawnee. He was relieved to see that Flanders and Thomas were not yet back from their hunting trip. Daniel was sure that when they got back to camp and found it deserted and saw all the footprints in the snow, they would know what had happened and would head back to Boonesborough to sound the alarm.

Late in the afternoon, Daniel and the other twenty-seven captured men arrived back at the Shawnee camp. Shortly after their arrival, a Shawnee warrior tried to force Daniel to carry a large copper pot for him. Angrily Daniel forced the pot back at the Indian, knocking him to the ground. The warrior scrambled to his feet, but before he could strike at Daniel, Chief Blackfish stepped between them, and the warrior turned and walked away.

The following morning Daniel noticed a group of Indians clearing a patch of land. It did not take him long to realize what they were doing. They were preparing ground for a gauntlet. Immediately Daniel went to Blackfish to complain. He reminded the chief that he had promised that his men would not have to run the gauntlet.

"This is not for your men. This is for you. You made no bargain for yourself," Blackfish told him.

Daniel was stunned, but he could not argue with Blackfish's logic. So he began to prepare himself. He knew that very often prisoners didn't make it out of the gauntlet alive.

Soon the Shawnee warriors formed themselves into two lines with sticks, clubs, and tomahawks in hand. Daniel, stripped to the waist, was led to one end of the double line, and then an Indian slapped him on the behind. Daniel sprinted as fast as he could, trying to stay out of range of the sticks and clubs of the warriors on one side while denying the warriors on the other side the space they needed to take a strong swing at him. By swerving from side to side rather than running in a straight line, Daniel made it to the end of the gauntlet with just a few cuts and bumps. When he was finished, he turned and shook hands with many of the Shawnee warriors, who were amazed at how easily Daniel had slipped through the gauntlet and how little harm they had been able to inflict on his body.

That night, Daniel slept soundly in a buffalo-skin blanket beside the fire. His men were alive, and he had survived the terrifying run through the Shawnee gauntlet. But the future was uncertain, and their lives were still in danger. When morning came, they would begin their long and dangerous march deeper into Indian territory.

Chapter 13

Big Turtle

The following morning the group set out. The Shawnees expected their captives to carry the cast-iron salt pots with them, and this caused the first problem along the way. Some of Daniel's men declared that they would rather be shot dead where they stood than carry anything for the Indians. But Daniel urged the men to think of their families and bear their captivity sensibly, looking for a way to escape as soon as possible.

There was only one man in the group who was not required to carry anything. His name was Andrew Johnson, a particularly small man but an excellent woodsman. At first Daniel could not understand the change that had come over Andrew. Andrew acted as if everything frightened him. He shut his eyes when a rifle was fired, and he insisted on staying in the center of the group at all times. Although he was given a pot to carry, he put it down and left it behind so many times that the Shawnees gave up and carried it themselves. After a while Daniel realized that Andrew was only acting stupid, probably because he was hoping the Indians would not watch him as closely and then he could escape.

Daniel hoped that Andrew would try to make a break as soon as it was possible. He wondered what might be happening back in Boonesborough. Undoubtedly Flanders and Thomas had gone back to the salt spring and realized that the men had been marched away. It would be puzzling to them as to why there were no signs of a fight, but Daniel was hopeful that by now the settlers at Boonesborough would know that the men were missing. It seemed to him, however, that there was little the settlers could do about it. It would be difficult enough for them to make it through the winter in the fort, much less mount a rescue attempt.

The going was not too difficult for Daniel and the nine other woodsmen in the group. It was the militiamen from Virginia who suffered the most. They were not used to eating the sap and bark from trees or remaining calm under the threat of impending death.

The group reached the Ohio River, which had not frozen over. The Shawnees used wide buffalo-skin boats to ferry them across the icy water. The boats were large enough to fit twenty men at a time into them.

Finally, ten days and over one hundred miles later, the hungry and freezing group arrived in the Shawnee village of Chillicothe, located beside the Little Miami River.

Chillicothe was laid out very much like an American fort, with several hundred homes inside a stockade. Some of the homes were traditional ones, made with bark and bent saplings, but others were more like settlers' cabins—log homes but without chimneys or windows.

As the men walked into the village, a cry went up and the women and children rushed out of their homes. Daniel and the other men were marched to a huge council house in the middle of the village and made to stand at attention while everyone inspected them.

Some of the Shawnees had set out a gauntlet beside the council house, and this time all of the prisoners were required to run it. However, because most of the warriors were weak from hunger and the exhaustion of the trek, they were unable to inflict any serious punishment on their captives. Samuel Brooks's broken arm was the most significant injury.

That night the Shawnees and their prisoners feasted on a hearty dinner of corn cakes and venison, after which the Shawnees required Daniel and the captives to "dance like long knives." It was a little difficult doing the Virginia Reel, especially without any music, but the men did the best they could. When they had finished, the exhausted and rather embarrassed men were taken to cabins and tied up for the night.

For the first time the men were alone together, and everyone's pent-up emotions boiled over. The men had been taken prisoner, marched over one hundred miles from home, been threatened with injury or even death in the gauntlet, and been humiliated by dancing for their captors, and now they were tied up. Some of the men argued bitterly against Daniel's decision to surrender them all at the salt licks. They insisted that they should have fought, even though they were outnumbered four to one, and, if necessary, died rather than giving in. Many wondered what would happen to them now; they had heard rumors about Indians brutally torturing their captives.

These conversations and the fears they evoked did not give anyone a peaceful night's sleep, and everyone was on edge the next morning when the men were once again led into the council room. This time the men were allowed to sit or squat along the walls as a succession of Indians milled about, looking the white men over. Some of the men had their muscles felt and their feet examined. Soon men were being led out of the room, some of them in groups and others individually. When about half the men had left, Pompey arrived and crouched next to Daniel.

"What will happen to the men who are going?" Daniel asked him.

"They are being adopted by the families who have chosen them," he replied. "Those families have lost husbands or sons in the recent wars, and they are replacing them with your men."

"Really?" Daniel remarked. He had heard about Indian adoptions before but had never really understood what happened, or why.

"Yes," Pompey said. "They will go through a ceremony where the new family will ask that their departed one's spirit be put into the new man, and then the new man will be part of the family for the rest of his life."

Daniel sat quietly watching the proceedings and thinking about what Pompey had told him. The Indians certainly had a different way of looking at people. He could not imagine a white family adopting an Indian.

Soon the room became quiet as Blackfish entered, wearing enormous copper earrings and draped in a bearskin that came to his knees.

Chief Blackfish walked directly over to Daniel.

Daniel scrambled to his feet.

"You were the one commanding the group following the kidnapped girls?" the chief asked.

Daniel gulped. Blackfish had said nothing about this on the journey from Kentucky. Daniel still vividly recalled the rescue of Jemima and the Callaway sisters. And he recalled that it was rumored that one of the Indians they shot dead was the son of a Shawnee chief.

"Yes, one of them was my daughter," Daniel said.

"And one of the warriors you killed was my only remaining son," Blackfish said, his eyes boring into Daniel.

Daniel stood still. The hairs on the back of his neck stood on end. He knew that if he said the wrong thing, he could be killed on the spot or, worse, be slowly tortured. He took a deep breath and began to speak. "Many bad things happen in war and are best forgotten," he said.

The chief stood stern and silent, and then his face broke into a smile. He slapped Daniel on the back. "Brave man!" he laughed. "All right. War is like that. When we are at war, I kill you and you kill me."

Daniel nodded in agreement, relieved at Blackfish's mild response. But he was stunned when he heard the next thing the chief said.

"You are a courageous man, and your reputation as a fighter goes before you. I have decided to adopt you as my son. You shall replace the one I lost that day."

Daniel tried to act calm, though his mind was racing. At forty-three years of age, he was being adopted, and by no less than a Shawnee chief! He hardly had time to dwell on the situation before three old women grabbed him by the elbows and, nodding and talking excitedly, led him down to the river. It was freezing cold as they stripped Daniel's clothes off him and pushed him into the Little Miami River. Daniel gasped for breath as they tore bark from a nearby tree and used it to scrub him all over. Within a minute or so, he was so cold he did not feel it.

When the women were done, they wrapped Daniel in a buffalo blanket and escorted him back to Blackfish. That was when the most painful part of the process took place. Blackfish plucked out almost all of the hair on Daniel's head, leaving only a scalp lock on the top. Daniel tried hard not to show how much pain he was in. Finally the ordeal was over, and Blackfish decorated Daniel's single lock with beads, silver ornaments, and feathers and then presented him with a breechcloth (loincloth) to wear. Blackfish then gave a speech that Pompey relayed to Daniel. In the speech, Blackfish said that Daniel was now the son of his heart and that he had nothing to fear because he had been adopted into a great family. Wherever he went, Daniel only had to say that he was the son of Blackfish and he would be given support and protection.

That night Blackfish provided a wonderful meal for the village, consisting of venison, corn cakes with maple sugar, bear fat, and hominy. By the time Daniel lay down for the night, he was totally exhausted and a little confused about how he felt. Part of him admired Blackfish and the community he had built around him. Daniel was now the son of a great chief. But he was also a captive, and he needed to get home to Boonesborough as soon as possible.

The following day Daniel moved into Blackfish's cabin. His new "mother" and two little "nieces" lived there. Daniel spent many hours with them, learning how to master the Algonquian language the Shawnees spoke.

On March 10 the sixteen men who had not been adopted by the tribe were marched out of the village and off to Detroit. Among them was Samuel Brooks, still nursing his broken arm. The Indians planned to hand the men over to the British for a twenty-pound bounty each. Daniel and Blackfish accompanied the group.

It was the farthest north Daniel had ever been, and he loved the changing scenery. It was spring, and wildflowers were beginning to bloom on the plains north of Chillicothe.

In Detroit the British gladly paid the bounty for the woodsmen and militiamen the Indians had brought them. The British governor pressed hard to buy Daniel as well. Daniel learned that this was because the British wanted him to return to Boonesborough and persuade the remaining settlers to abandon that region of Kentucky altogether. However, since Daniel was also Big Turtle, son of Blackfish, there was no way the Indians were going to hand him over, and so he returned to Chillicothe with the Shawnees.

When they got back, Daniel was informed that Andrew Johnson had escaped. One night Andrew had stolen a gun, hunting knife, blanket coat, and ammunition and slipped into the darkness. His adoptive parents were very concerned for him, since he had continued his half-witted act and convinced them that he did not even know which way was south. Daniel, on the other hand, was sure that Andrew would make it back to Boonesborough and spread the news about the fate of the men.

Daniel knew that it would not be so easy for him to escape. Blackfish made sure that he was watched at all times. At first, when they went hunting, Daniel was given only one measure of powder and one bullet so that he would not be tempted to slip away from the hunting party. After a while Blackfish allowed him two shots, and then three. Daniel started to keep a little of the powder from each loading and store it in the hem of his shirt. Sometimes he was able to recover a bullet from a dead animal before the others arrived to search for it. Better yet, he soon showed his skill at fixing rifles and became the gunsmith for the village. Some of the guns were irreparable, and Daniel found that he was able to secret away an unstocked rifle barrel and a lock. No one missed the items, which he hid in a thicket behind his cabin.

Although Daniel knew he had a good chance of evading the Shawnees, he decided to stay with them until he could find a way to help all of the men escape together. He could not imagine returning to Boonesborough without the others. This plan was dashed, however, when Daniel learned that Blackfish was planning a raid on Boonesborough toward the end of June. Now Daniel knew he had get back to Boonesborough and warn the settlers, and he had a better chance of escaping if he went alone.

His opportunity to escape came on June 16, 1778, when he accompanied a group of Shawnee men and women on a trip to get salt from a nearby lick. Just after dawn that day, the men spotted a flock of wild turkeys and gave chase. Daniel was told to stay with the women and lead the packhorse forward. Seeing his chance, Daniel quickly cut the buffalo-hide tugs that held the packs on the horse and let them fall to the ground. Then he jumped onto the horse and galloped away. As he did so, he heard his adoptive mother calling, "Don't do it, Big Turtle. They will catch you and kill you."

Daniel tucked his head down and urged the horse on. Although he figured he had at least a half-hour lead, he knew the Shawnee were quite capable of catching up. He rode as fast as his horse would take him. When his horse could not gallop any longer, Daniel let the animal go and continued on foot, doing his best to hide his tracks. He ran through brushwood, jumped over boulders, and waded down creek beds.

When darkness prevented Daniel from going any farther, he sank from exhaustion into a deep sleep until he felt something grabbing at one of his toes. His heart pounding, Daniel sat up. *Had the Shawnee caught up to him?* With relief, Daniel saw that it was nothing but a mischievous fox, and he quickly fell back asleep.

When he awoke at sunrise, his feet ached from the previous day's running. Daniel had no time to lose, so he put his moccasins back on and continued heading south.

All the next day and the day after that Daniel traveled. By then he was quite hungry, and he judged that he was out of danger of being followed. Now all Daniel needed was some food.

As he pressed on farther south, Daniel felt safe enough to make a fire near the Blue Licks spring, where their troubles had begun several months before. His Indian and wilderness skills came in handy in the discovery of roots and berries, and he thought as he ate that nothing had ever tasted so delicious. Soon, Daniel trotted off on the last leg of his journey back to Boonesborough. He was finally almost home! The thought of reuniting with his family kept Daniel moving as fast as he could. He had no way of knowing that what awaited him was actually much more hostile than what he had just escaped.

Chapter 14

Three Paths

"It's me, Daniel Boone," Daniel yelled over and over. He was within three hundred feet of the settlement now, and the last thing he wanted was to be mistaken for an Indian and shot. Slowly, and still yelling, Daniel approached the gate to the fort, which swung open for him. Inside settlers stood in stunned silence.

"We thought you must be dead by now," one of them spluttered.

"Well, bless my soul, you made it back," said another.

"Did you bring the others with you?" asked a third.

Soon everyone was crowded around Daniel asking about family members and friends who had been taken hostage at the salt lick. Some of the people became upset when they realized that Daniel had escaped on his own and that he could not even tell them where some of the captured men now were. Daniel explained that he had returned alone to warn them of an impending Indian attack. A few of the settlers felt Daniel had made the wrong decision when he had his men surrender, but they were also glad that the man they depended on for their safety was back.

As the clamor calmed down, Daniel scanned the group for Rebecca. When he could not locate his wife or any of his children, he asked what had happened to them.

"Gone back east," one of the women said. "Rebecca was sure you had been killed, so she took the children and went back to stay with her father."

Daniel gulped. Although he had been away for six months, this was far less time than he had been gone on some of his hunting trips. Being taken prisoner, however, changed everything. He had never before given Rebecca any cause to suspect that he wouldn't make it home—until now.

Daniel returned to his cabin. A few sticks of furniture were still inside, along with a half-whittled toy canoe that he and Daniel Morgan had been working on before he went off to the salt lick. The family cat slipped in the door and jumped up on Daniel's knee.

"Look's like it's just you and me," Daniel said as he stroked it.

Just then the door flung open, and there stood Jemima.

"Papa!" she yelled with her arms outstretched.

"Jemima!" Daniel ran to embrace his daughter. "Thank goodness there is at least one friendly face here!"

Daniel soon learned that Jemima and Flanders Callaway had refused to leave with the others. His daughter had stubbornly held out hope that he was alive and wanted some family member to be in Boonesborough to welcome him back.

As the days went on, most of the settlers came to understand that Daniel had taken the course of action that would save the most lives at the salt lick—and probably theirs as well. They were willing to heed Daniel's warning that a huge attack was about to take place, and they followed his advice on how to prepare for it.

Soon men were replacing sections of the stockade that were rotten and completing the last two corner bastions so that they would be able to defend the fort from all four sides. The women pooled their food supplies so that everyone could see exactly how much food they had on hand to endure a siege. Daniel realized that the water supply would be cut off if the Indians surrounded the fort, so he ordered several teenagers to craft cisterns from hollowed-out logs. It was a laborious job, and it went much slower than Daniel would have liked.

Under the circumstances, every man in the settlement needed to bear arms, regardless of whether he was a slave or freeman. When the number of men was totaled, it came to sixty. Twelve women and twenty children were also living in the fort.

On July 17 Daniel was guarding the fort when he heard a faint cry from across the river. It sounded like someone calling out in English, so he gathered several men together and cautiously went to investigate. The men crossed the river by canoe and found a naked man lying in the bushes. The man looked barely alive. When Daniel looked closely at him, he realized that it was William Hancock, one of the captured men who had been taken to Chillicothe and adopted.

One of the men took off his shirt and draped it around William, and then the men carried him back to the canoe and into Boonesborough. Daniel took him to his cabin and cared for him until he regained his strength.

The story William told was amazing. After Daniel had escaped, the other adoptive families became very suspicious of their white sons and were careful not to let them out of their sight. William told Daniel that his adoptive father slept in front of the door and made him sleep naked so that he would not escape. Nonetheless William became desperate to get home when he heard that four hundred Shawnee warriors and some soldiers were about to descend on Boonesborough.

Nine nights before, William had decided to make a break for it, clothes or no clothes. When his Indian father went to sleep, William managed to step over him and pry the door open far enough to sneak out. William grabbed three pints of corn mush from a gourd outside the cabin. He then headed for the horse pen, took one of the horses, clambered onto the animal's back, and galloped away. When the horse gave out at the Ohio River, William made a raft out of logs tied together with grapevines. The raft slowly fell apart as it carried him twenty miles downstream and deposited him on the south bank of the river. The weather was cloudy, and without the sun or the stars as his guide, William did not know which way to go. He ate the last of his corn and could not find any other food. Exhausted and starving, he gave up all hope of making it back to Boonesborough and lay down to die.

As he lay there, he spotted a tree with some markings on it. He crawled over to it and, much to his amazement, found that the name "Stephen Hancock" was carved into the tree. That was his brother's name. Then William recalled that the summer before, he and his brother had camped about four miles north of Boonesborough. During the stay Stephen had carved his name into a tree.

Now that William knew where he was, he knew he could find his way back to Boonesborough. With renewed energy he hobbled on until he came to the Kentucky River, where he hollered out for help.

The news that four hundred warriors and soldiers were gathering for an attack shocked Daniel. It was four times the number he had imagined would come, and he encouraged all the settlers to redouble their efforts to make the fort safe. He also wrote a letter to the Virginia militia asking for help:

Dear Colonel,

Enclosed is my deposition with that of Mr. Hancock, who arrived here yesterday. He informed us of both French and Indians coming against us to the number of near four hundred, whom I expect here in twelve days from this. If men can be sent to us in five or six weeks, it would be of infinite service, as we shall lay up provisions for a siege. We are all in fine spirits, and have good crops growing, and intend to fight hard in order to secure them. I shall refer you to the bearer for particulars of this country.

I am, & etc. Daniel Boone

With the letter dispatched, all Daniel could hope was that the Indians would delay long enough so they could harvest their corn. The settlers reported seeing Indian spies from time to time, but the spies did not disturb the fort.

Toward the end of August, everyone's nerves were frayed. The corn was gathered and dried, and still there was no sign of an attack. Daniel decided that the best thing to do was to strike first and attack the Indians in their own villages before the Indians could attack them. He proposed that a posse attack Paint Creek Town and steal the Indians' horses and provisions.

Richard Callaway, Flanders Callaway's uncle, spoke out against the idea, saying that Daniel was mad for planning to leave the fort less protected at such a time. They disagreed publicly about the right course of action, and Richard was even angrier with the men who volunteered to go along with Daniel.

On August 31, Daniel led a group of thirty men out of the fort and north toward the Indian settlement. They had gotten as far as the upper Blue Licks spring when eleven of the men lost their courage and declared they were turning back.

Daniel let them go, knowing that scared men do not fight well. The other nineteen men marched on with Daniel. When they were about five miles from Paint Creek Town, Daniel sent Simon Kenton on ahead as a scout. About an hour after Simon left, gunshots rang out. Daniel and the others raced to see what had happened. They arrived just in time to see thirty warriors, some on horseback, others on foot, descending on Simon. A single dead Indian lay over a log. Daniel ordered his men to attack, and a ferocious skirmish followed. Soon two of the warriors were badly hurt, and the other Indians retreated, dragging the wounded men to safety. They left behind three horses and all of their baggage.

Fearing that the Indians might return to avenge the death, none of Daniel's men wanted to linger for long. They quickly fled, taking the horses the Indians had left behind.

The men made camp about three miles away while Daniel considered what to do next. He decided to send two men to spy on the village. Simon and Alex Montgomery offered to go, and

Daniel sent them off with a warning to stay out of sight at all cost. The two returned before nightfall with good news and bad news: The good news was that no one would be pursuing them, since there were no warriors in the village, only women and children. The bad news was that the warriors were probably on their way to Boonesborough.

Daniel ordered the men to be ready to move out at first light in the morning. He knew it would be disastrous if the Shawnees arrived at Boonesborough before he and the men got back.

The following morning the men were as eager to leave as Daniel was. Daniel urged everyone to be as quiet as possible and to keep watch for any signs of Indians. The men made it to the lower Blue Licks spring before they caught a glimpse of them. Daniel was surprised to see that not only were there four hundred Indians consisting of Shawnee, Wyandots, and Cherokee warriors but also marching with them was a regiment of forty Detroit militiamen, mostly French-Canadians carrying a British flag. Daniel knew that the presence of the militiamen would make any encounter even more complicated. The British were very interested in ridding the frontier of colonial settlers and had sided with the Indians.

Daniel signaled his men to leave the path and head into the undergrowth, giving the Indians a wide berth. They were not spotted and made it back to Boonesborough on September 6. Judging by how close behind the Indians were, Daniel was sure they would attack the fort the next morning.

During Daniel's absence, Squire, along with two of his sons, Moses and Isaiah, had arrived at the fort. Daniel was glad to see them and was grateful for the extra ammunition they had brought with them.

The next morning, Monday, September 7, 1778, was warm and sunny. It would have been a great day for hunting or fishing, except for one thing—the Indians were coming. Daniel, who was patrolling the outskirts of the fort around midmorning, was the first to spot them. The Indians marched over Hackberry Ridge south of Boonesborough and down onto the river flat.

Within minutes all sixty men in the fort were at their stations, ready to fire on Daniel's order. However, the attackers stopped about three hundred yards from the fort in a grove of peach trees. Daniel watched as the French-Canadian soldiers trimmed the branches off several trees, leaving a single upright tree in the middle of the grove. Then the soldiers threw some sewn-together buffalo skins over the top to form a makeshift canopy. Daniel recognized his adoptive father, Blackfish, in the group who assembled under the canopy.

Half an hour after their arrival, one man stepped forward from among the Indians holding a white flag. He began to walk toward the fort. Daniel recognized him immediately. It was Pompey, who climbed onto the cornfield fence and called, "Captain Boone, Captain Boone."

"I am here," Daniel replied.

"We have come to accept the surrender of the fort. We expect you to keep your word, which you gave when we captured you. We have a letter from Governor Hamilton promising you safe conduct to Detroit."

The leading men in the settlement gathered around Daniel.

"Ask to see the letter," one of them suggested.

Several others nodded.

Before Daniel could yell back, he heard another voice. "Sheltowee, Sheltowee [Big Turtle in Algonquian]." Daniel recognized it instantly as Blackfish's voice.

"Your father wants to talk to you," Pompey yelled. "Come and meet him."

"All right. I will walk to that tree stump, and he can meet me there," Daniel called, pointing to the spot. The tree stump was only sixty yards from the fort, well within the range of the settlers' rifles.

Daniel had mixed feelings about seeing his adoptive father again. Although Daniel had considered himself a prisoner, Blackfish had considered Daniel to be his son, and he had loved Daniel and treated him well. Daniel was not sure what kind of greeting to expect from Blackfish, nor was he sure how to proceed. When he was captured, Daniel had led the chief to believe that the fort would surrender. He had given his word on it. But Daniel knew that the settlers would not easily give up their homes and community.

Daniel opened the gate and walked out. He stood at the tree stump and watched as Blackfish and several other Indians left the canopy and came to meet him.

"Hello, my son," Blackfish said, extending his arm.

Daniel grasped his hand. "Hello, Father."

One of the other Indians produced a panther skin for Daniel and Blackfish to sit on. Three young boys fanned the two men with leafy branches.

When they were seated, Blackfish looked intently at Daniel. Tears were streaming down his face. "My son," he said, "what made you run away from me?"

Daniel found it difficult not to cry, too. He had, in a strange way, grown to love Blackfish. Now they were again face-to-face, and his adoptive father had missed him. "I had to," Daniel finally replied. "How else would I ever see my wife and children again?"

Blackfish shook his head. "You could have asked me and I would have let you go."

Before Daniel could respond, another Indian walked up to them. Daniel knew he was Chief Moluntha, a powerful Shawnee chief. The chief's face looked like thunder.

"You killed my son the other day over on the Ohio River," Moluntha said accusingly.

Daniel tried to stay calm. He had no idea that Simon had killed such an important person.

"I haven't been to the river in a long time," he lied. "It must have been someone else."

"No," Moluntha boomed. "It was you. I tracked you back to this place."

Daniel could feel his pulse race as he waited to see what would happen next. Not only had he been responsible for the death of the chief's son but also he had lied in the presence of his father. Both deeds carried harsh penalties in Shawnee culture.

After a long pause, Blackfish waved his hand. "There are other things to discuss," he said. "What is done is done." He paused to pull out a letter from his leather pouch. "This is the letter from Governor Hamilton."

Daniel took the letter and quickly read it. It was much as he had expected. The governor reminded Daniel of his agreement to surrender the fort, and he promised pardon and safe passage to Detroit for all the settlers. The British would honor claims for lost property, and if the enlisted men among them joined the British army, they could maintain their previous ranks. The letter ended with a warning. If the settlers chose to resist, the British would not be held responsible for their safety.

When Daniel put the letter down, Blackfish passed him a beaded belt.

"See this wampum belt," he said. "One end of it represents Detroit, and the other end Boonesborough. The rows of beads between them represent various paths. The red path is the warpath and is the path we came by. The white path is the path we can walk along together as we return to Detroit. And the black path is the path of death—the path you will walk alone if you do not surrender."

Daniel stared at the belt, wondering whether he had the right to choose the black path for himself and for everyone else inside the fort. If he could just stall for time, he might not have to make that decision. He hoped that the militia reinforcements were on their way and would arrive any day to put an end to the standoff. Finally he came up with an excuse that he thought sounded reasonable.

"I will take the papers and the belt back to my people," he said, "but I cannot speak for them anymore. I was gone so long that other chiefs have risen among them, and they must be consulted."

Much to Daniel's relief, Blackfish nodded. He understood that leaders rise and fall.

"In the meantime," Daniel said to Blackfish, "I know your people are hungry. Take the cattle that you need, and we will send corn out for you."

Blackfish smiled. "And I have brought a gift for your womenfolk."

He signaled one of the warriors, who presented Daniel with seven smoked buffalo tongues.

Daniel thanked the chief, and the two men shook hands and parted. As he walked away, Daniel began to doubt that he and his adoptive father would ever meet on such friendly terms again.

Chapter 15

Under Siege

Once he was back inside the fort, Daniel showed the letter from Governor Hamilton to the men. Richard Callaway was incensed that Daniel had ever given the impression that Boonesborough would surrender. Daniel tried to explain that it had been the only way he could think of to appease Blackfish, but Richard would not accept this explanation. He accused Daniel of plotting with the British for the downfall of Boonesborough, and he even suggested that while sitting outside with Blackfish, he had once again promised they would all soon surrender.

The accusation was not true, but arguing about it at that moment was not a wise use of their time. Daniel managed to turn the conversation back to the situation that faced them. Should they defend their homes to the death, or should they surrender peacefully and accept the offer of safe passage?

"I'll shoot the first man who tries to surrender!" Richard yelled when it became clear that some of the men were seriously considering it.

Daniel insisted that the men should vote to see which option they should take. The men voted unanimously in favor of fighting. No one asked the women and children what they thought.

"Well," Daniel said when the vote was over. "I guess I'll die with the rest of you."

Even though the men had decided to fight, Daniel still hoped the Virginia militia would arrive at any moment. Determined to do whatever he could to stall for time, he called for Pompey to arrange a meeting in the late afternoon.

At the appointed time for the meeting, Daniel, accompanied by Bill Smith, one of the men of the community, marched out of the fort. In an attempt to fool the Indians into thinking there were more men in Boonesborough than they had reckoned, Daniel had the women and older girls put on men's clothes and mingle around the gate to the fort when it was opened.

The meeting with Blackfish started on a cordial note. The three men smoked a pipe together and engaged in pleasant conversation. Things turned ugly, however, when Bill told Blackfish that the settlers did not wish to surrender. Blackfish could scarcely believe what Bill had said. Daniel tried to smooth things over by saying that their minds were not fully made up and that they should talk some more. Blackfish agreed, but he did not look happy about the situation.

As the men departed from the meeting, Daniel offered to make a feast the next day for the most important warriors. Blackfish agreed to this offer, and they both agreed that their men would come unarmed.

All night and the following morning, the women of the fort made food while the men manned the bastions. By three o'clock everything was ready. The men carried tables and chairs outside the fort, along with their wives' best pewter ware. Then they brought out the food, a mouth-watering selection of venison, buffalo, corn, greens, cheese, milk, and bread. Daniel's secret aim was not only to stall for more time, but also to show the Indians that they had plenty of food in the fort and did not fear a long siege.

Everyone appeared to enjoy the feast, and afterward Blackfish announced that he wanted another meeting with the leading men in the fort. Eight men, including Squire Boone and Flanders and Richard Callaway, followed Daniel to the meeting area. The Indian warriors outnumbered the settlers two to one, a fact that made Daniel feel uneasy. Daniel was glad he had ordered sharpshooters to stand ready at the bastions and shoot at the first sign of trouble.

The men talked for some time. Eventually, Blackfish announced that he would allow the settlers to live in peace, in accordance with the agreement they had reached with the Cherokees before the founding of Boonesborough. This all seemed a little too quick and simple to Daniel, who was on his guard when Blackfish stepped forward to embrace him. Other warriors also made moves toward their white counterparts. Suddenly Daniel heard Richard yell, "No, get your hands off me!" A shot was fired from the fort, and then mayhem broke loose.

Blackfish lunged at Daniel, who tripped him and pushed him to the ground. All around Indians and white men were fighting. One Indian fell to the ground, shot through the head. Another warrior brought his tomahawk down on Daniel, who ducked quickly enough that the brunt of the force from the tomahawk blow fell on his shoulder and not his head. Daniel felt warm, sticky blood begin to seep through his clothing as he looked around for the others. Flanders and Richard were already sprinting for the gate to the fort, and two other men were close behind them. Daniel dodged a warrior and followed them.

Within five minutes only one settler was unaccounted for. The gate was shut, and each man took his prearranged position. The horses and cows inside the fort went wild with the sound of gunfire, galloping around their enclosure. Most of the women and children barricaded themselves in a storeroom in the middle of the stockade, though a few of the braver ones, like Jemima, ran messages from bastion to bastion for the men so they could coordinate their defense.

After the initial volley of gunfire, there was a lull in the fighting, and Daniel was able to make the rounds of his men. He found Squire, his shirt soaked in blood, slumped over his gun trying to reload it with one hand.

"It's my shoulder," Squire said. "I took a bullet when we were running for the fort, and I think it's still in there."

Daniel wiped his hands on his buckskin pants and felt around the wound. "I'm gonna' have to use my knife," he said as he made a deep incision.

Squire groaned as Daniel hit the bone with the point of his knife.

"Here it is," Daniel finally said, fishing out the bullet with his forefinger and thumb.

Squire tried to stand up, but he could not, and Daniel ordered some of the men to carry him to his bed.

"I'm not going without an ax," Squire yelled. "If any of the Indians scale the wall, I'll defend myself to the death."

Jemima had a bullet wound, too, but it was only a graze, and she was able to go on helping the men.

The gunfire went on until nightfall, and the men then took turns manning the bastions to watch for Indian activity. The following morning the shooting started again, and Daniel guessed that the Indians and their British helpers had no shortage of bullets. Still, the longer the fighting went on, the more encouraged the settlers were. The fort had held for twenty-four hours; maybe it could hold until reinforcements arrived.

The Indians, however, obviously needed some way to breach the walls, and they had several possibilities. They could tunnel under them, blow them down with cannon fire, or set them on fire. It did not appear that they had any cannons with them, so that left tunneling or fire. On the third night the settlers heard rustling outside the wall. As they peered over the wall into the darkness they saw the shapes of Indians piling flax against the stockade wall. Minutes later the pile burst into flames.

"Let me handle it," John Holder yelled as he raced for the gate.

The other men covered him as he grabbed a large bucket of water and slipped out of the fort. Shots rang out from the trees, but John kept running. He threw the water onto the fire and then scampered back inside the gate. The fire was out, but the men spent the rest of the night watching for another one.

Apparently the Indians did not want to try the same thing twice, because they turned their attention to something else. The next morning those in the fort became aware of chopping and digging sounds. Whatever was causing it was out of the line of sight of the fort, but there was a telltale streak of muddy water in the Kentucky River.

"They must be digging upstream along the riverbank," Daniel told Flanders.

Flanders nodded. "That's about the only thing that could stir up that mud. God help us if they tunnel under the fort."

This was not a possibility that Daniel was eager to divulge to the others. The settlers had enough to worry about without the thought of Indians coming up under their feet!

That night the Indians hurled burning balls of bark into the compound. Most of them landed in the yard and were quickly stomped out. The women stood by with long poles to pry any burning shingles off the roofs of cabins. Meanwhile, with his good arm, Squire quickly converted some old rifle barrels into squirt guns and gave them to the children to water down the roofs so they would not so easily catch fire.

While the strategy of pelting the fort with burning balls of bark did not do any serious damage inside Boonesborough, it was devastating to the Indians. To hurl the burning bark over the stockade walls, the warriors had to get very close to the fort, where the fire they were carrying silhouetted them against the darkness. One after another they were shot down, until no more came.

The Shawnees then turned their attention to a small fence that was joined to the back wall of one of the cabins. They set fire to it, obviously hoping it would spread to the cabin wall, which was part of the stockade. A slave named London bravely volunteered to put out the fire. He ripped the fence away from the cabin wall, but sadly he was shot and killed in the process.

The fighting continued day and night for another nine days, by which time everyone in the fort was exhausted and hungry. The constant digging noise only added to the people's fears, as they had no way to gauge where the tunnel would come up or when the Indians would break through into the fort. Worse still, Daniel feared that the Indians might load the tunnel with gunpowder and blow the fort apart.

Each day Daniel eagerly scanned the horizon for any sign of reinforcements, but in the end it was nature that came to their aid. On the night of Thursday, September 17, the Indians launched a particularly strong assault on the fort. They shot rifles and hurled more fireballs. This time the children had to scramble onto the cabin roofs and put the fires out. Daniel feared they would not be able to hold on much longer.

Just when everything seemed hopeless, storm clouds began to gather overhead. Soon it started to pour with rain, dousing the fires and repelling the Indian attack. As lightning lit up the night sky, Daniel spotted a new trench leading toward the fort. For a moment he wondered what it was, and then he knew. The heavy rain had caved in the tunnel.

The residents of Boonesborough held on through the night, and as dawn arrived, they saw the Indians and the Detroit militiamen packing up their camp. Boonesborough was saved! It was several days before the last Indian left the area. Daniel left the fort and tracked the last of them across the river and thirty miles into the forest. Then, convinced that the retreat was not just a trick, he jubilantly returned to Boonesborough.

That night the settlers dined on cabbages and other vegetables from their gardens. They examined the walls of the stockade and pulled 125 pounds of bullets from the outer logs. It had been quite a siege—the longest in Kentucky's history.

A week after the siege ended, reinforcements arrived from Virginia. With the fighting over, many of the men decided to stay on as settlers.

Even while the siege was in progress, Richard Callaway, Daniel's friend and his daughter's uncle, had been questioning Daniel's decisions. But Daniel was shocked when he received a letter telling him that Richard was accusing him of treason. The charges were that he had handed the men over to the British and that he had conspired to deliver the entire settlement of Boonesborough to them as well.

It was a great blow to Daniel. His heart was heavy as he wrote a letter to the officers of the militia court defending his actions. His defense was simple: He had done everything he could to save as many lives as possible and buy time while they waited for reinforcements. The court questioned the other men, including William Hancock, who had managed to escape from Chillicothe. Each of these men backed up Daniel's account of the events, pointing out that the Shawnees would have overwhelmed them and that Daniel had taken the "wise, safe and prudent course" of action given the situation.

The court found Daniel innocent of all charges, but it was a bitter time for him, and a permanent rift developed between the Boones and the Callaways.

Once the court-martial was behind him, Daniel left Boonesborough and headed east to see Rebecca and the children. Jemima and Flanders Callaway went with him. They arrived in the Yadkin Valley in North Carolina on November 5, 1778. Rebecca was so shocked to see Daniel that she was speechless. She and their five children still living at home were settled in a small cabin on her uncle's farm. Six additional children—the orphaned sons and daughters of Rebecca's uncle, James Bryan—were living with her as well.

Daniel built a larger cabin for them, and the entire family, including Jemima and Flanders Callaway and Susannah and William Hays and their two children, who were living nearby, all moved in together.

While he had been away in Kentucky Daniel's mother had died. Other changes had taken place as well. The Revolutionary War was raging on. General George Washington, whose bravery as a colonel in the Virginia militia had so impressed Daniel during the failed attempt by the British to capture Fort Duquesne twenty-four years before, was valiantly leading the patriot forces. Military campaigns in the struggle for independence had now spread to Georgia and South Carolina. It seemed to Daniel that the entire South was in an uproar. Families were divided, with some backing the patriot cause and others, nicknamed Tories, supporting the British. Some areas became so unsafe for Tories that many asked Daniel to help them emigrate to Kentucky. They told him they feared the Indians less than they feared their patriot neighbors.

During the winter of 1778–1779, Daniel hunted in the Blue Ridge Mountains, and in the spring and summer he prepared to lead another group through the Cumberland Gap to Kentucky. At first Rebecca was not at all interested in returning to Indian country, and she and Daniel had many arguments about what the family should do. Eventually, however, she agreed to go, and in mid-September a group of one hundred people left the Yadkin Valley bound for Boonesborough. The six motherless children Rebecca had taken in went with them as well.

Most of those in the group walked, while a few young children and women rode horses. The weather got cooler as fall arrived, and the rivers were icy cold. Still the group remained in good spirits and arrived in Boonesborough on October 28, 1779, without any major incidents.

Depressing news about the remainder of the salt licks captives awaited Daniel. Although some of those in Shawnee hands had managed to escape, the prisoners who had been turned over to the British were being treated poorly. Samuel Brooks had died from lack of attention to his broken arm, and two other prisoners were seriously ill. Daniel noted with some irony that it was much better for a white man to be held prisoner by Indians than by the British.

Daniel's stomach lurched when he saw Richard Callaway again and recalled the humiliation of the court-martial. In Daniel's absence, Richard had gained a firm control of life in Boonesborough. With all that had happened between them, Daniel knew that it would be impossible for him to live in Boonesborough as long as Richard was in control.

Instead Daniel led a group of new settlers six miles northwest, where he planted the new settlement of Boone's Station. The founders of this new settlement included Daniel's married daughters Susannah and Jemima and their families, and his brothers Samuel, Jonathan, and Edward and their families. They made their way to the site of their new community without any idea of just how difficult the approaching winter would be.

Chapter 16

A Deadly Trap

A foot of snow was already on the ground as the Boone clan and about ten other families set down their belongings on the bluegrass plain. They built lean-tos out of forked sticks and rough-hewn boards. In even an ordinary winter this would have provided dubious protection from the cold, but this winter was the coldest anyone could recall. Many of the cows and horses froze to death, and the wild turkeys grew too weak to move and died on their perches. Hunting was a trial because the men's frozen hands made it impossible most of the time for them to load their rifles. The cold weather and meager diet made several people ill, and as February approached, some of the people even died.

In the spring those who were strong enough tilled the land and planted corn and tobacco. They also built a fort to prepare for more Indian raids. Daniel put in a claim for land and was granted a four-hundred-acre tract around Boone's Station. To earn money, he hired himself out to survey other people's tracts of land. He was in high demand because he knew more about the lay of the land west of the mountains than any other white man.

As spring progressed, forty-one-year-old Rebecca made the surprising announcement that she was expecting another baby early the following year. Still, she took charge of the household while Daniel was away on his surveying trips.

While Daniel was away on one of these trips, a force of three hundred militiamen from Kentucky crossed the Ohio River and attacked Blackfish in Chillicothe. The militia lost nine men in the raid, and the Shawnees lost two. One of them was Blackfish himself, who died from an infection around a bullet wound. Daniel was deeply saddened to hear of his Indian father's death, and he wondered how or when the fighting would stop.

In a counterattack, the Indians ambushed a convoy on the Ohio River. The convoy was on its way to New Orleans with pelts and other trading goods. Forty people were killed in the attack, and others were taken hostage.

The round of violence continued when a British army unit, aided by the Indians, brought a cannon into the Ohio Valley. Using it to blow holes in the stockades, the soldiers and Indians forced the surrender of two small communities, taking over three hundred prisoners in the process.

There were more bloody battles, and life on the frontier became a nerve-wracking experience. In October 1780, a year after arriving at Boone's Station, Daniel and his brother Edward were returning from making salt at the Blue Licks spring. About halfway back, they stopped to allow their horses to graze beside a creek. A walnut tree caught Edward's attention.

"Let's crack some of them," he suggested.

Daniel felt uneasy. "I don't think that's a good idea. There could be Indians nearby."

"I don't believe there's an Indian within a hundred miles of this place," Edward laughed as he walked over and reached for some walnuts.

Edward had just begun cracking the walnuts between two stones when Daniel caught sight of something out of the corner of his eye. It was a bear heading off into the woods.

"I'm going after the bear. Keep a good lookout," Daniel said as he reached for his gun.

Daniel followed the bear a short distance and then brought it down with a single shot. He was making sure the animal was dead when he heard gunshots. He dropped to the ground and crawled back to the stream. A grisly sight met him. A group of Shawnee warriors surrounded Edward's dead body. Daniel watched as one Indian announced, "We have killed Daniel Boone."

Many people had told Daniel over the years how much he and Edward looked alike, but he never imagined that Edward would be killed in his place.

Daniel quietly slipped away and headed for

Boone's Station, where he told his sister-in-law Martha the distressing news that she was now a widow with five children to look after.

Four months later Rebecca gave birth to their tenth child, a son they named Nathan. Within a month of Nathan's birth, both Susannah and Jemima gave birth to daughters, adding further to the Boone clan.

Daniel was elected to represent Kentucky in the Virginia legislature, which was scheduled to meet in Richmond. He arrived in Richmond on May 7, 1781, just as the British army under General Charles Cornwallis was advancing toward the town. The legislature was reconvened in Charlottesville, Virginia, and that meeting had to be disbanded after hearing that General Cornwallis had sent British soldiers to capture the members of the legislature. Frustrated, Daniel gave up and headed home for a summer of hunting and planting.

In the fall the second session of the legislature was called, and Daniel headed east once again. On October 19, 1781, while Daniel was still in Richmond, General Cornwallis surrendered the British army to George Washington at Yorktown, Virginia. The patriots had won.

The British, however, retained control of Canada and still wanted to dominate the "unclaimed" lands of the Ohio Valley. Wearily, Daniel realized that the Revolutionary War might be over in the east but the fighting in the west would continue.

He was right. In March 1782 three hundred militiamen headed north across the Ohio River and attacked a peaceful village of Delaware Indians. Ninety-six of the Indians, over sixty of them women and children, were killed. In retaliation a fresh outbreak of Indian raids followed. In August a rumor began to circulate that the English and Indians were again on their way to the Boonesborough area. Simon Girty, a white loyalist who had sided with the Indians, was said to be leading the group of raiders.

The rumored attack did not occur, but things moved quickly when Daniel, now a colonel in the militia, received word that Bryan's Station, a small settlement to the north, was under siege. Daniel quickly rallied forty-five men, who galloped northward to help. Under Daniel's command were his son Israel; his nephews Tom, Squire, and Sam Boone; and his son-in-law Peter, along with Peter's brothers, Abraham and Joseph Scholl. Along the trail they met up with militiamen from other Kentucky settlements on their way to help, including men from Harrodsburg, Boonesborough, and the new settlement of Lexington. Together they arrived on August 17, 1782, at a spot overlooking Bryan's Station only to find that no Indians were in sight. The siege was over, and the Indians had moved on.

The 182 militiamen descended the hill and camped outside Bryan's Station. Now the question became, what should they do next? Among the group were four officers, Colonel Stephen Trigg, Major Hugh McGary, Colonel Daniel Boone, and Colonel John Todd, a Virginia lawyer. Todd was the ranking officer and he decided that rather than wait for the reinforcements on their way north, they should pursue the Indians right away. He ordered Daniel to pick up the trail of the Indians so they could all follow it.

It did not take Daniel long to get the feeling that something was very wrong. Although there were few footprints, suggesting that he was pursuing a small group, each footprint was deeply embedded in the muddy ground. This led Daniel to conclude that the Indians were walking in single file, being careful to tread in their leader's footprints. The campsites along the way backed up this conclusion. The fires there were much too large for a small group.

Something else just didn't seem right. The trail was much too easy to follow. The Indians had left discarded items and broken branches along their route. This, Daniel concluded, could mean only one thing: The Indians wanted to be followed, and were leading the militia into a trap.

The militia stopped on the south bank of the Licking River near the Blue Licks springs on August 19. There the river took a sharp bend, and as the scouts moved ahead and rounded the bend, they spotted a small number of Indians standing in the sun smoking pipes.

Colonel Todd called the officers together for a council. When they were all assembled, he asked Daniel, "What do you think this means?"

"Colonel," Daniel replied, "up to five hundred of them are hidden just ahead of us, and they intend to fight us."

"How do you know that?" the colonel asked.

"On account of the easy trail they left us to follow and the size of their fires. I think there are about five hundred of them. The men we see are luring us to fight them, and then the others will appear. I know this country like the back of my hand, and I can tell you that if we move forward now, there will be nowhere for us to take cover. We must not take the bait and fall into the trap they have set for us."

Major McGary of Harrodsburg, whose mind had been clouded with rage since his stepson was killed by Indians five years before, stepped forward and stood nose to nose with Daniel. "What nonsense!" he snapped. "We have enough force to whip all the Indians we can find. What is this about, Boone? I never saw any signs of cowardice in you before."

Daniel felt rage growing within him. "No one has ever dared call me a coward before!" he yelled back. "I can go as far in any fight as any other man."

With that McGary shouted, "Then prove it," as he raced for his horse and charged into the river. He waved his rifle over his head and yelled, "Them that ain't cowards, follow me!"

The men watched in stunned silence for a moment, then McGary's Harrodsburg Company jumped on their horses and charged off after their leader.

Colonel Todd turned to the remaining men. "Mount and follow," he ordered.

Daniel's men turned to him to see if they should obey the colonel's command.

Daniel could not see any alternative to obeying the colonel. "Come on," he said. "We are all slaughtered men."

Once they crossed the Licking River, McGary had the sense to stop his men and wait for the others to catch up. They then divided into three formations, with Colonel Trigg commanding the right wing, Todd the center group, and Daniel the left wing. It was decided that most of the men should proceed on foot.

Cautiously the militiamen began the half-mile trek up the hill ahead of them. Just as the first men reached the summit, there was a deafening war whoop, and Indians surged over the hill. Others appeared from behind bushes and rushed up the ravines. A volley of gunfire broke out, and the first twenty militiamen fell to the ground dead.

Daniel, aware of how outnumbered and ill prepared they were, was still obliged to fight the best battle he could. As he urged his men up the hill, an Indian popped up from behind a stump. Daniel took aim with his rifle, shooting the Indian dead. Boone's men leaped over the body and continued on up the hill.

Suddenly, from out of nowhere, Major McGary came riding up. "Boone, why aren't you retreating?" he yelled. "Todd's and Trigg's lines have given way, and the Indians are surrounding you."

Daniel turned and looked down at the river. No one was guarding the horses, and the Indians were running toward them. It would be only a matter of a minute or so before the mounted Indians were upon them. Daniel knew he had to act quickly.

"Men!" he yelled. "Stay together and go left into the woods. Cross the river upstream. Go! Go!" Then he turned to the four men nearest him. "Stay with me, and we'll fend them off for as long as we can while the others get away," he said.

The rest of the men ran for the trees, or so Daniel thought until he realized his son Israel was still at his side. A riderless horse galloped by, and Daniel grabbed its reins. "Get on it and flee!" he shouted to Israel.

"Father, I won't leave you," Israel declared.

Daniel turned to see how close the Indians were, and a second later he heard a moan. He swiveled around just in time to see his son fall to the ground. Daniel dropped to his knees and stared at the gaping wound in Israel's neck. He had no doubt that the wound was fatal.

It was obvious that a sharpshooter was close by. Daniel grabbed the horse he had intended for his son's escape, jumped on its back, and urged it on. He leaned forward until he was flat against the animal's back, making him a more difficult target.

A horrific sight met Daniel at the river. The water was clogged with floating, bloodied bodies. He plunged his horse into the river as bullets fell all around him. Reaching the other side, Daniel found the rest of the Boone Company huddled together, partially hidden by a stand of trees.

Daniel scanned the group, immediately noting that his nephew Tom was missing. Another nephew, Squire, had made it across the river, but his pelvis was shattered. A quick head count revealed that six men of the company were missing. There was no point in waiting for them. Daniel was sure that anyone still on the other side of the river was either dead or mortally wounded.

"Follow me down this trail," he said, pointing to an old buffalo trace. "Our best chance is to make a run for Boone's Station."

The men, some struggling to help their wounded comrades, headed back to the settlement. The Indians did not pursue them.

When the men arrived home, the women and children of Boone's Station were waiting anxiously in the safety of the fort. Daniel then had the heart-wrenching job of telling Rebecca that Indians had killed a second of their sons.

Five days later the men returned to the site of the battle to bury the dead. Vultures and the summer heat had combined to make it the grisliest scene Daniel had ever witnessed. Daniel didn't think he would ever get the images out of his head.

Later, when General Clark reviewed the battle plans, or lack of them, he blamed Major McGary for touching off the attack and Colonel Todd for not controlling McGary. But in his heart Daniel blamed himself. He could not stop the men from entering into an ambush, the result of which was that six of them, including his own son, now lay in a mass grave on a hill beside the Licking River.

The Battle of Blue Licks, as the ambush came to be called, was one battle too many for a lot of the Kentucky settlers. Once again they fled in droves, willingly exchanging their land, crops, and cabins for packhorses to carry them to safety in the east.

For his part, Daniel once again wrote begging for reinforcements from Virginia. "If something is not speedily done," he wrote, "no doubt [Kentucky] will be wholly depopulated. I have encouraged the people here in this country all that I could, but I can no longer encourage my neighbors nor myself to risque [sic] our lives here at such extraordinary hazards."

Chapter 17

Limestone

Before the next round of violence could begin, a messenger arrived in Boone's Station. The one word on the piece of paper tucked into his hat said it all: "PEACE." It was true. After much wrangling, Great Britain had signed articles of peace that secured the independence of the United States and ceded control of the western lands, including Kentucky, to the fledgling nation. The news was greeted with mixed feelings in the Boone household. Two of Rebecca's uncles had been North Carolina loyalists. One of them was believed to be killed, and the other had been sentenced to hang but ultimately was freed in exchange for an American prisoner. Yet British policy had encouraged the Indians to harass and kill many of the settlers, a policy that had led to the death of Daniel and Rebecca's own son.

Still, everyone was agreed on one thing: It was good that the war was finally over. Without the British influence, relations between Indians and settlers had become more peaceful. With that, the Boone family moved a few miles westward to Marble Creek.

The end of the war and the peace treaty led to a new wave of settlers headed to Ohio, not through the Cumberland Gap, but down the Ohio River from Pittsburgh, Pennsylvania.

As Daniel thought about this, his saw a new opportunity. Many of the settlers landed at the town of Limestone, Kentucky. Although the settlement had only twelve houses at that time, Daniel was sure it was about to grow rapidly. His friend Simon Kenton had started the settlement and was eager to have Daniel as one of its leading citizens. Daniel agreed to move there.

Daniel's announcement that the household was moving led both nineteen-year-old Levina and sixteen-year-old Rebecca to marry the young men they had fallen in love with. Levina became Mrs. Joseph Scholl, and Rebecca became Mrs. Philip Goe. This left fourteen-year-old Daniel Morgan, nine-year-old Jesse, and baby Nathan to make the journey with their parents. Rebecca was less than enthusiastic about moving so far away from her newly married daughters, but she faithfully packed up the cabin and loaded its contents onto packhorses.

Once settled in Limestone, the Boones became prosperous almost immediately. Daniel was right.

Thousands of settlers flooded into the settlement, sometimes as many as one hundred a day, and they all needed a place to stay, advice on where and how to buy or lease land, and provisions to set up a household.

Within weeks of arriving, Daniel and Rebecca opened a general store and tavern. The store sold flour, salt, corn, beef, pork, dry goods, and housewares. Daniel also bought items from passing traders, mainly skins, furs, ginseng root, and corn whiskey, which he shipped upriver to be sold in Pittsburgh. The tavern had rooms in the back that were hired out to weary travelers. The general store and tavern were instantly popular, and Daniel's seven slaves worked full-time to keep both establishments running.

Daniel was sworn in as a deputy surveyor of Fayette County and as a county sheriff. The surveying soon became a family business, and Daniel returned to Marble Creek to persuade other members of the family to join him. Joseph and Levina and their children moved to Limestone, as did and Jemima and Flanders. All three sons-in-law helped with the various facets of surveying, while Daniel Morgan and Jesse acted as chainmen. Daniel was pleased to finally be in a situation where he could help his children earn a good living.

About a year after his move to Limestone, Daniel met a man named John Filson. John was a thirty-year-old schoolteacher from Chester County, Pennsylvania, who had used money from his father's estate to buy land warrants in Kentucky.

He had no farming skills, and he planned to write a book that would encourage people to migrate to Kentucky, thus allowing him to sell his new land holdings and make a good profit.

The first time the two men met, John plied Daniel with questions about his adventures. At first Daniel was reluctant to talk about them as it sounded like bragging. But John was a persistent young man, and soon Daniel found himself answering all of his questions as best he could. It was the only way Daniel could think of to get John to stop asking them!

October 22, 1784, was Daniel Boone's fiftieth birthday. It was also the day a particular book was published. The book was entitled *The Discovery, Settlement and Present State of Kentucke...To which is added An Appendix, Containing the Adventures of Col. Daniel Boon.* John Filson had an ambitious fifteen hundred copies of the book printed in Wilmington, Delaware, and Daniel received a copy by special courier six weeks later.

Although most of the information in the book was correct, John had written the book to sound like an epic myth, with Daniel as the hero who had single-handedly opened up the west. John had used the language and thoughts of a schoolteacher and put them into Daniel's mouth. Daniel laughed as he read that when he saw the rugged passes of the Appalachians, they reminded him of the ancient cities of Persepolis and Palmyra. He had no idea where these places were. Despite the flowery imagery, Daniel liked the book and hoped it would indeed encourage more people to come to Kentucky. The book also contained much information on Kentucky, and many of those who passed through Daniel's tavern had read it and were eager to talk to the man behind the story.

Ironically, at the same time that Daniel's story was encouraging more migration, Daniel was himself again having trouble over land. Somehow he was too trusting and never quite closed all the loopholes in a deal. In 1783 he had met a man named Gilbert Imlay, a retired army officer. Daniel "sold" him the rights to a large tract of land he owned. Unfortunately for Daniel, he registered the sale to Gilbert before he received a deposit for the property from him. Once the transfer was registered, the land became Gilbert's, even though he never paid Daniel a penny for it. Gilbert sold the land for cash right away, and Daniel lost all claim to the land.

This was only one of many legal predicaments Daniel got into over land deals. He continued to trust people and did not recognize a swindler when he saw one. To make matters worse, many of the land claims he surveyed became known as "shingle tracts." This meant that one claim overlapped another like shingles on a roof. Sometimes as many as seven or eight people would all have what appeared to be the legal title to the same piece of land. Even though Daniel was a careful surveyor, he used only the most basic equipment, and like most other surveyors, he found himself embroiled in many lawsuits.

In the midst of these crises Daniel had long become something of a folk hero. John Filson's book had also been published in England, France, and Germany. Now people from all over the world had heard of his exploits and fame. The original book was rewritten to read more like a diary. John Trumbull published this new edition, which became an instant best-seller, making Kentucky seem like a wonderful place to settle in. More white people continued to settle in Kentucky, and Indian tribes from north of the Ohio River continued to resist. Conflicts became increasingly violent.

In the face of such constant attacks, the settlers in Kentucky became outraged when the Virginia legislature failed to send more men and ammunition to help defend the settlers. There was talk that Kentucky should secede from Virginia and become part of either the British or the Spanish empire. Even when faced with such angry threats, the Virginia legislature was slow to send aid, and so the people of Kentucky decided to make their own unauthorized attack against the Indians.

On September 29, 1786, eight hundred militiamen under the command of Colonel Benjamin Logan began making their way across the Ohio River. Daniel was in command of one of the companies of men as they began making their way north toward a complex of four Shawnee villages located on the headwaters of the Mad River. The men arrived at the villages at noon on October 6, catching the Indians by surprise. In fact, many of the warriors were away defending several other villages on the Wabash River that they suspected were going to be attacked.

On seeing the militiamen, the Indians raised an American flag to signal that they had peaceful intentions. But it made no difference to the men from Kentucky, who raced into the villages with their swords drawn and guns blazing.

Most of the Indians in the villages managed to flee into the woods to safety, and few Shawnees or militiamen were killed in the battle. However, the militia took a number of Indian prisoners, among them Chief Moluntha and Nonhelema, the sister of Cornstalk, who had been on a mission of peace at Point Pleasant when he was killed by colonial zealots. Nonhelema was a female chief and a woman of very high standing among the Shawnee, so much so that the colonists referred to her as Queen Nonhelema.

In the late afternoon, after the fighting was over, Daniel, his old friend Simon, and several other militia officers sat around a fire with Chief Moluntha, Queen Nonhelema, and several of the other Indian prisoners, talking and smoking a pipe (a ritual on the western frontier that often occurred after a battle). As they sat talking and passing the pipe, Major McGary, whose hotheaded antics had led the militia into the deadly trap at the Battle of Blue Licks, burst into the circle, incensed that Daniel and the other officers were sitting and talking with the Indians. McGary stormed over to Chief Moluntha and demanded, "Was you in the Battle of the Blue Licks?"

Moluntha had not been anywhere near the battle, but he seemed to misunderstand the question. With a smile on his face, he politely nodded.

"Then I'll give you Blue Lick pay," McGary screamed, pulling a tomahawk from his belt and plunging it into Chief Moluntha's head, killing him instantly.

Daniel could scarcely believe what he had just seen. The other Shawnees recoiled, fearing they too would be killed, as several officers raced to physically restrain McGary. In a complete rage, Simon leaped to his feet and attacked McGary. When he pulled his knife to kill the man, he also had to be restrained.

The next day, sobered by the horrible events of the night before, the militiamen and their hostages returned to Kentucky, and although Shawnee warriors followed them, they were not attacked.

Back in Limestone, Daniel was put in charge of housing and feeding the Shawnee prisoners. He converted a warehouse into a barracks and kept the prisoners under guard. They stayed there until the following February, when Daniel released two of them, a French-Canadian trader and his Indian wife. Daniel supplied the couple with horses and provisions and instructed them to find the Shawnee chief and ask him to come to Limestone and work out a prisoner exchange plan. Over the years, in the course of their raids, the Shawnees had taken hostage many settlers, though no one knew the exact number, and many of these hostages still lived among the Indians. Now Daniel wanted to use the prisoners the militia had taken as leverage for the safe return of these captured settlers.

On March 4, 1787, Noamohouoh, a Shawnee chief, came to Limestone with an offer from Captain Johnny, who had become the paramount Shawnee chief following the death of Chief Moluntha. Noamohouoh brought along three white children who had been captured when their parents were killed. He said he had brought them to demonstrate the Shawnees' sincere desire to exchange prisoners. In return Noamohouoh asked for the immediate release of Queen Nonhelema as evidence that the settlers were also sincere. Noamohouoh told Daniel that when the Queen was returned to him, he and Daniel would go to Captain Johnny together and bring all of the white captives the Shawnee nation was holding back to Limestone.

Daniel believed that the Shawnees were acting in good faith, but none of his fellow militia officers agreed with him. They all thought it was a trick and that the three small children were a poor ransom for a Shawnee queen. However, Queen Nonhelema was no longer in Limestone. She had been transferred to a prison in Danville, south of Harrodsburg, where Daniel tried to negotiate her freedom. Despite some heated letters from Daniel, Colonel Patterson, who oversaw the prison, refused to release her.

In the end Daniel had to promise Colonel Patterson that if Queen Nonhelema was released, he would be personally responsible for making sure that Captain Johnny kept to his word. In late

March the queen was finally brought to Daniel's tavern in Limestone and then allowed to leave with Noamohouoh.

In mid-August Captain Johnny and seventy-five Shawnee warriors appeared on the riverbank opposite Limestone. As a gesture of trust, Daniel sent his nineteen-year-old son Daniel Morgan and two Indian prisoners over to greet them. All went well, and the next morning Daniel, Colonel Logan, and some of the men who had missing wives and children ferried themselves across the river to meet with the Shawnee chief.

Both Colonel Logan and Chief Johnny made long speeches, which one of the men transcribed. The leaders on both sides then signed the transcripts. The Indian chief made a mark as his signature, and then the white prisoners were brought out.

Most of the prisoners were women and children, and some had been with their Indian captives for so long that they were stunned to think of leaving them. Daniel watched as one man found his wife among the group. The woman had sad eyes and never said a word as the man embraced her and led her back to the river. Another man spotted his daughter, who had been captured by the Indians as they crossed through the Cumberland Gap. The daughter was now married to a Shawnee warrior, and she wept bitterly as she was parted from her husband and reunited with her father. Many of the small white children clung to their Indian mothers, and their own fathers had to pull them away and drag them back to the ferry kicking and screaming.

When the prisoner exchange was over, one little girl remained. Daniel bent down to talk to her. "What is your name?" he asked in his best grandfatherly voice.

"Chloe Flinn," she replied.

Daniel was relieved. At least she was old enough to remember her European name, a sign that she probably had not been with the Indians for too long.

"Where are you from?" he asked.

Chloe's lip trembled as she replied, "Ma and Pa have a cabin with flowers by the river. But I don't know where they are."

Daniel's heart went out to the little blonde girl in front of him. He scooped her up. "Come on, Chloe," he said. "I'll take you home with me, and my wife will fix you corn cakes and molasses. There are lots of children to play with, and I'll try to find out where your parents are."

Chloe put her arms around his neck and clung to him.

Daniel then ordered the Indian prisoners to be ferried across the river and returned to their own people.

That night Chloe made herself at home at the Boones' tavern, and the next day Daniel set about finding what had happened to her parents. The search took three months, but eventually he learned that Indian raiders had attacked a farm owned by a Flinn family in western Virginia. The father had been killed in the raid, and the mother, two daughters, and a son were separated by the

Indians and marched off to different towns. Sometime later there was news that the mother had died and the other two children had been taken farther west with their captors. Chloe was the only member of the family to be returned in the prisoner exchange. With this information Daniel was able to locate an uncle of Chloe's and returned her to him. It was a satisfying moment for Daniel, though he had grown quite fond of the little girl and was sorry to see her go.

The following year, 1787, Daniel was once again elected to the Virginia Legislature. In the previous two years, over twelve thousand people had entered Kentucky, and they wanted a voice in the affairs of their government. Their first concern was the same as it had always been—the safety and security of the settlers. In the past four years, Indians had raided countless cabins, killed three hundred settlers, and stolen thousands of horses. The people of Kentucky expected Daniel to get the legislature to take their needs seriously.

While Kentucky was growing rapidly, planters, merchants, and lawyers had more sway over the state budget than the lowly farmers who had risked their lives to settle the land. As a legislator, then, Daniel was not entirely successful. By the end of his term in the Virginia legislature, Daniel was sure of one thing—the frontier was calling him again.

Chapter 18

The Lure of Open Spaces

Daniel, Rebecca, their three youngest sons, and one slave moved eastward to Point Pleasant, at the confluence of the Ohio and Kanawha Rivers. Although it was located farther east, the area was much more isolated and less settled than Limestone.

In Point Pleasant Daniel cut logs and built a snug cabin for his family. Then he set up a small store and trading post. His plan was to spend more time hunting and less worrying about local and state affairs. However, Daniel was well known, and before he knew it he had been elected as one of two representatives for the area to the Virginia legislature.

In September 1791 Daniel, accompanied by Rebecca and ten-year-old Nathan, journeyed to Richmond for the legislative session. It proved to be a landmark session, with the Kentucky delegation voting to separate from Virginia and petition to the federal government to become the sovereign state of Kentucky.

In the midst of the momentous debates that surrounded this decision, Daniel managed to find time to show Rebecca and Nathan around Richmond. They picnicked on roasted oysters on the banks of the James River and strolled together through the bustling cobbled streets.

Daniel was particularly eager to see more state militiamen stationed along the Ohio River. He petitioned the Virginia Council for a contract to transport ammunition for the new troops and supply them with food and other provisions. The request was granted.

When the council's session ended just before Christmas, Daniel sent Rebecca and Nathan home with the other representative from the Kanawha area. Daniel himself set out for the state armory on the Potomac River. He was issued four hundred pounds of gunpowder, sixteen hundred pounds of lead, and a keg of flints. His job, according to the contract, was to supervise their delivery to the militia companies stationed in the Shenandoah Mountains and along the Monongahela and Wheeling Rivers. Snow and ice made the job maddeningly slow, and it was April before Daniel got back to Point Pleasant.

Although Daniel was committed to delivering supplies and ammunition to militia companies, he encountered criticism and difficulty along the way.

In the end, the experience soured him on government contracts, and once again he sought to live a simpler life.

Daniel wound down his trading post and store and moved with Rebecca to a squatter's cabin sixty miles up the Kanawha River, near Fort Lee. Eleven-year-old Nathan did not make the move with them but went to a Baptist boarding school in Lexington to finish his education. The family slave was sold, and for the first time in their married lives, Daniel and Rebecca lived alone.

This was the life Daniel had always wanted—he and his wife dependent on no one but themselves and their survival skills. There was just one problem: Daniel was now fifty-eight years old, and the rigorous life he had led had taken its toll on his body. He could no longer run through the forest as he used to, jumping over boulders and scampering down creek beds. In fact, it was not uncommon now for him to suffer bouts of rheumatism that were so painful he could barely lift his feet off the ground. Still, Daniel would not give up. Rebecca often went with him on his hunting trips to keep camp and melt down the bear grease. On one occasion Daniel killed over 150 bears in less than a month. He sold the bear grease from these animals for a dollar a gallon, and this, plus the money from the sale of the bearskins, provided the couple with enough money to live comfortably.

In 1794 Nathan joined his parents on the Kanawha River. At thirteen years of age, he had finished his formal schooling. Daniel decided it was time to teach his youngest son how to survive in the wilderness. Their first outing, however, nearly proved fatal. They had been camping for about five days when they crossed the river in search of a particularly large buck that Daniel had spotted on the far bank the day before. They were unable to track down the animal, and just as they were about to recross the river, Daniel heard the sound of wood being chopped. Instantly he knew what it was. Indians must have discovered their camp and were making a raft to follow them across the river.

Daniel motioned for Nathan to be quiet and follow him. Silently they climbed into the canoe, with Nathan lying flat in the bow. Then Daniel grabbed a paddle, and with hardly a ripple, he began to make his way down the river under the cover of overhanging trees. Through the branches he caught a glimpse of a raft crossing the river upstream. On it sat eight warriors. Thankfully, the Indians did not spot Daniel and his son as they glided downstream.

The near encounter with the Indians scared Nathan so much that he begged his parents to move back onto the bluegrass plains. Although Daniel was happy living on the Kanawha River, he did not know if he and Rebecca would be able to bear losing a third son in an Indian attack, so he eventually agreed to move.

From time to time, Daniel heard news of what was happening in American politics, but it did not make him yearn to be a part of it again. He was, however, relieved to hear of the Treaty of

Greenville. Despite ceding control of the western frontier to the United States at the end of the Revolutionary War, the British tried to hold onto Ohio. They built forts on U.S. territory in the region, and as they had done before, they enlisted the help of the Indians to fight for them. Backed by the British, the Indians had pulled off many daring raids and twice defeated federal forces sent to quell their activities.

Finally, in 1794, President George Washington ordered General Anthony Wayne to take a large force into the area and negotiate a treaty with the Indians. Wayne led an army of three thousand men, made up of regular army soldiers and Kentucky militiamen, into Ohio. At first the Indians scoffed at his efforts, but then on August 20, 1794, Wayne's forces routed over a thousand Indian warriors at the Battle of Fallen Timbers. After this battle, the Indians' will to fight began to wane. Eventually, in August 1795, they agreed to a treaty. The agreement was called the Treaty of Greenville, and in it the twelve Indian tribes in the region agreed to open up all of Ohio to white settlement.

The family moved to Brushy Fork in 1795, located near the Blue Licks springs. Daniel Morgan owned a tract of land there, and he gladly allowed Daniel, Rebecca, and Nathan to build a cabin on it. Once again Daniel set out to make a living for his family, planting corn in springtime and hunting for bears in the fall. Other game was now hard to find, and Daniel often thought back to the time when deer, buffalo, and bears in abundance roamed the area. Now not a single buffalo remained in Kentucky, and Daniel hardly ever saw signs of deer.

At Brushy Fork Daniel and Rebecca were now surrounded by four daughters and their growing families. And Nathan was much less afraid there, helping Daniel during bear-hunting season. In 1797 the Boones moved to the mouth of Little Sandy Creek, living a simple life among family and friends until 1799, when once again the lure of open spaces and plentiful land was too much for Daniel to resist.

Although he was nearly sixty-five years old, Daniel felt he had one more move left in him. This particular move would take him right out of the United States and into the Spanish territory of Upper Louisiana. The Spanish and English had been at war for two years, and the Spanish were afraid that the English, who had taken over much of Canada, would attack Upper Louisiana from the north. To discourage such an attack, Spanish Lieutenant Governor Zenon Trudeau encouraged more families to settle in the Spanish territory. He did not care if they were American families, as long as they would fight the British for their land and "officially" practice the Roman Catholic religion. In reality, the governor did not even care what religion the settlers practiced, as long as they worshiped in private homes and did not try to build churches.

American settlers entering the region were offered large land grants at no cost, but were required to build a cabin and cultivate the land.

Daniel was offered more land than most settlers because the Spanish governor recognized his leadership qualities, which he hoped would inspire thousands of men to follow in Daniel's footsteps.

Daniel Morgan Boone, who was just as footloose as his father, had made several forays into Louisiana and had located a lush valley along a creek called the Femme Osage. The soil there was rich, and the wooded areas nearby provided an abundance of game. Daniel Morgan's description of the place set Daniel's heart leaping, and Daniel announced that he would be leading a group west into Louisiana in September of 1799.

Daniel and Nathan had much to do before they set out. They felled an enormous poplar tree, from which they made a canoe sixty feet long and five feet wide. The Boones' belongings were loaded into the canoe, and Daniel Morgan and Nathan were designated to paddle it. Sixty-year-old Rebecca Boone would be their passenger.

Daniel's brother Squire, who had been living in New Orleans, was also eager to set out for Upper Louisiana Territory. He would be one of the men to man one of the boats with women and children. Squire's wife, Jane, however, refused to move yet again, and so she stayed behind.

The Kentucky group set off for Limestone, paddling down the Licking River and then up the Ohio. In Limestone they met up with more people who would be part of the group, including Susannah and William Hays and their seven children, and Jemima and Flanders Callaway and their ten children, plus several young single men. The other three Boone children, Jesse, Levina, and Rebecca, decided not to go along. All in all, fifteen households were making the trip to Louisiana, most of them related to Daniel in some way.

Nearly all of the women and children planned to travel by canoe, while the men and some hired slaves drove horses, cattle, and hogs along the river's edge. The whole group caused quite a commotion as final preparations were made.

Just as they were about to set out from Limestone, eighteen-year-old Nathan came to Daniel with a special request. He wanted to turn back! It was not until he left Little Sandy Creek that he realized he loved sixteen-year-old Olive Vanbibber and desperately wanted to ask her to be his wife. Now, Nathan told Daniel, the thought of leaving Kentucky without her was agony to him.

Daniel and Rebecca liked Olive, and they helped Nathan to get a marriage license and sent him on his way back to Little Sandy Creek. Nathan promised to meet them in Femme Osage if Olive agreed to marry and go with him.

With Nathan dispatched, the group set out. They planned to drift down the Ohio River, paddle up the Mississippi to St. Louis, and then along the Missouri River to Femme Osage Creek. They reached the Mississippi in the first week of October. Daniel then led his family into St. Louis, where the lieutenant governor of Louisiana, Don Charles Delassus, greeted him with military honors. Daniel was delighted to be so honored, and even more delighted when he learned that the lieutenant governor was preparing to make the area of Femme Osage a separate administrative district, with Daniel as its "Commandant." Daniel would now serve as civil administrator, military commander, and judge. In short, he would be in charge of interpreting and enforcing the laws in the new settlement.

Because Daniel was very impressed with the efficiency of the Spanish administration (he thought the Virginia legislature could well take note of their methods), he agreed to become the commandant. His only concern was that he had heard that in order to claim Spanish lands, the owner had to farm them for a year and build a cabin and fences. Daniel feared that being a commandant could make him too busy to fulfill these requirements. When he mentioned this to Don Charles Delassus, the lieutenant governor understood the problem immediately. He promised Daniel that he was exempt from complying with the farming rule.

With all the arrangements taken care of, the group journeyed on, crossing the Femme Osage Creek and traveling another two miles through the Missouri River bottoms, to where Daniel Morgan had chosen land. Daniel was delighted with his son's choice of land, and his job as the commandant was to allocate the particular plots.

Daniel had just begun the long process of allocating land when there was a death in the group. Daniel's thirty-nine-year-old daughter Susannah had taken ill toward the end of the journey from Kentucky and never recovered. Susannah's body was sadly laid to rest in a community cemetary. The rest of the relatives agreed to help look after her seven children.

The surveying and allocating of land took several weeks to complete, but in the end almost all of the community seemed content with their lot.

Daniel had just finished the job when Nathan and his new bride, Olive, arrived on horseback. They had made the trip alone, eating dried corn and the game that Nathan shot. Daniel was proud of the young couple and felt sure that sixteen-year-old Olive would fit right in to the frontier lifestyle and make a great wife for his youngest son.

Soon another wedding took place in the Boone family. Daniel Morgan married Sara Lewis, a fourteen-year-old American girl from Bon Homme, a settlement not far from Femme Osage. Now all six surviving Boone children were married.

In the spring Daniel and the other Boone men went trapping, and they were able to make a good income from trading the pelts of the animals they caught. Meanwhile the women and children farmed the rich lowlands, and there was always plenty of food to go around.

One of Daniel's unexpected pleasures in moving to Femme Osage was learning that many of the Shawnee and Delaware Indians from Chillicothe, where he had been held captive and adopted by Blackfish, had also relocated to the area. In fact, they had established a small settlement at the mouth of the Borbouse River. The settlement was called Rogerstown after their leader, Jimmy Rogers. Jimmy and another white man, Joseph Jackson, had chosen to live among the Indians. Joseph was, in fact, one of the men who had surrendered with Daniel to Blackfish and the Shawnees at the upper Blue Licks spring. When given the chance to leave the Indians, Joseph had chosen to stay and thrown his lot in with them. In the winter months, when it was too cold to hunt, Daniel liked to visit Rogerstown and reminisce about old times.

One day one of Daniel's grandchildren asked him if he was afraid to sit among the warriors. Daniel looked the child in the eye and said, "While it may have been necessary to fight them, I am very sorry that I ever killed a Shawnee. They have been kinder to me and kept their word more often than the white people I know."

The next two years passed quietly, and Daniel was pleased with the decision to move to Louisiana. The only dark spot was learning that Levina, who had stayed back in Kentucky, had died after a short illness. Soon after, her husband, Joseph, emigrated to Femme Osage with their eight children.

All around the Boone enclave, though, things were changing. In 1803 President Thomas Jefferson purchased the entire midsection of the North American continent from France. The French had regained control of Louisiana two years before, when Napoleon Bonaparte forced the Spanish to sign the territory over to him. Once again Daniel Boone found himself living on American soil.

The French authorities, and then the Americans, asked Daniel to keep his position as commandant, and in 1804 Daniel had to carry out a duty that saddened him greatly. In December Daniel's son-in-law William Hays, the widower of his daughter Susannah, was shot and killed. It was not a stranger who shot him, but William's own son-in-law James Davis, who was married to Daniel's granddaughter Jemima.

Daniel and William had been on numerous hunting trips together and entered into many land deals as well. In the previous year, though, William had fallen into a deep depression over his wife's death and drank heavily. Daniel learned that it was during one of his drunken rages that William argued with James in his cabin. Seeing how drunk William was, James fled and hid in a tree. William followed him out of the cabin with his gun cocked and shouting that he could see James hiding in the tree and that he was going to shoot him in the head right then and there. James, seeing no alternative, aimed his rifle and shot William in the chest. William died a slow and painful death.

Daniel sent the case on to the court in St. Charles, where James was acquitted of the charges against him. However, the incident jarred Daniel's sense of family, and he mourned the loss of his son-in-law, friend, and father of seven of his grandchildren.

The following year news reached Femme Osage that Daniel's daughter Rebecca Boone Goe had also died. She was only thirty-five and left behind seven children. Daniel Morgan rode back to Kentucky and brought back the five oldest children to the Boone settlement. It was a difficult time for both Daniel and Rebecca. Of their four daughters, only one, Jemima, was still alive.

Eighteen hundred and six was not a good year for Daniel either. His mind and body were weary, but he had one last battle to fight. It could be summed up in three words—the Louisiana Purchase.

Chapter 19

"I Have Tried to Do Right"

President Thomas Jefferson had pledged to protect the land claims in Louisiana that were made under Spanish and French rule as long as the claimants could produce witnesses and paperwork to prove they were the rightful owners.

On February 13, 1806, Daniel Boone appeared before the U.S. commissioners in St. Charles. He had proof of his concession grant and a survey certificate stating that the former Spanish lieutenant governor of Louisiana, Don Charles Delassus, had granted him an exception to the building and farming requirement. Daniel had asked for this exemption because he did not think his duties as commandant would allow him the time to build a cabin or develop the land as he should.

At first the commissioners were inclined to let Daniel keep the land, but as more and more irregularities emerged in other cases, the commissioners took a hard line—they would not honor the exemption.

Daniel and his sons fought the ruling and appealed to the U.S. Congress, but it was no use. So in 1809 Daniel submitted a new petition asking for 10,000 acres of land. In the petition, he stated that he had never been rewarded for the great service he had given to his country, service that allowed so many to migrate and settle new land and to improve their way of living. In the end, Daniel's request was granted, but due to a misunderstanding, he received only 850 acres, the same amount he had been denied years before.

Daniel bore the disappointment as best he could. He still loved to hunt, and when his health permitted, he went off into the forest. At times when he was too weak to make it all the way home, he would stop off to rest at a close relative's place, and his son Nathan would be sent for to take him home.

By 1809 even Daniel had to admit that he was seriously ill. Rebecca talked him into moving to St. Charles, where he could be near a doctor. Jemima's son John Boone Callaway was a businessman in the town, and Daniel and Rebecca stayed with him. While Daniel was there, John persuaded him to dictate his autobiography to him. The exercise revived Daniel's spirits, especially when he thought about the role he had played in opening up the West to settlers.

By spring Daniel felt well enough to return to Femme Osage. The following fall two of Daniel's old Kentucky friends, Michael Stoner and James Bridges, came to visit. They told Daniel that they were on the way north to hunt beaver. Daniel could not resist the urge to join them, and the three of them, along with Flanders Callaway, William Hays Jr., and two slaves, set off up the Missouri River. They traveled all the way to the Yellowstone River, trapping and skinning beavers all the way. It was spring six months later when they returned laden with valuable furs packed in canoes. The trip proved to be Daniel's last long hunt, but it gave him many satisfying memories to think back on over the next few years.

From 1805 on, Daniel contented himself with living in a small cabin on Nathan and Olive Boone's property. It was there that Daniel first heard the news of war between the United States and Great Britain. The fight, which became known as the War of 1812, began as the result of long-standing disagreements between the British and the Americans over trade rights and the forcing of American merchant sailors into the British navy.

Most of the battles of the war occurred near the U.S. northern boundary with Canada, with the British navy blockading the entire Atlantic Coast, using their ships as bases from which to attack Washington, D.C., and also New Orleans.

In Missouri Territory (the part of Louisiana in which the Boones lived) Daniel witnessed events that reminded him of the Revolutionary War over three decades before. The British armed the Indians, and skirmishes once again broke out between the Indians and various militias and U.S. army soldiers. Once more Daniel was called to protect his family while his sons and grandsons were away in the militia.

One night Daniel received word that British-backed Sauk Indians were planning a massive attack along the Missouri River where the Callaways lived. This time Daniel did not think it was safe to stay, and he advised everyone to evacuate to the fort Daniel Morgan had built. His daughters-in-law and Jemima followed his advice and started to pack up important family papers and other possessions, strapping them into canoes. Flanders and the slaves were then given the responsibility of guiding the canoes downriver to the fort while the Boone clan rode there on horseback.

When Daniel and the family arrived at the fort, they waited for Flanders, the slaves, and the Callaway men to show up. Hours passed, and Daniel began to worry that they had been caught in an Indian attack. Everyone was greatly relieved when late in the evening the group finally did show up, although they brought bad news. The canoe with the only copy of Daniel Boone's autobiography had capsized, its prized possession lost.

In late winter of 1813 the Boone clan decided to make their traditional trip upriver to the Callaway sugar grove to make sugar, despite the fact that most of the men were away fighting. They had been camped in the grove for about three days when Rebecca began to complain about not feeling well. She had hardly been sick a day in her life, and Daniel became very alarmed. He placed Rebecca in a covered couch called a litter and carried her back to Jemima's cabin. The family did what they could to comfort her, but Rebecca continued to grow worse. She died a week later, on March 18, 1813.

Daniel chose her burial site, a grassy knoll along Tuque Creek that looked out over the rolling Missouri countryside. When he died he would be buried beside his wife of fifty-seven years.

Nearly two years later, in early 1815, another family tragedy occurred. Jemima's son James, one of Daniel's favorite grandsons, was a captain of a company of U.S. Rangers and was killed in an Indian attack along with five other men. What made the men's deaths even more tragic was that the Indians, who were acting as British agents, were unaware that an armistice had been signed and that the war was over.

With the war over, life became more predictable. Daniel spent a lot of time reflecting on his Quaker upbringing. Although he had not attended church regularly since his father had left the Friends Meeting in Exeter, Pennsylvania, as an eighty-year-old widower he now felt drawn to read his Bible.

Daniel also spent many happy hours recounting his adventures to his delighted great-grandchildren and entertained the many visitors who came to catch a glimpse of a living legend. Someone even came to paint his portrait. It was the first time

Daniel had ever seen a likeness of himself, and he thought it was too bad that he had waited until he was a scrawny old man to have one made.

Daniel lived with various members of the family, and in the late summer of 1820, was staying with Jemima and Flanders, who had moved near the village of Charette, which was farther from St. Charles. Daniel suffered through several bouts of fever there before he decided to return to Femme Osage.

Daniel's doctor and grandson-in-law John Jones advised against the trip, but Daniel was determined to go "home." Eventually he persuaded Jemima to let him go, and Daniel made the trip in a carriage.

Back at Femme Osage, Daniel was proud of his son Nathan's newly completed stone house. It was the most impressive in the area, looking like a Pennsylvania mansion. Olive cooked Daniel a special meal, and many friends and relatives came by to greet him.

The next day Daniel went riding with some of his grandchildren to inspect the corn crops. He arrived back at Nathan's house around midday, complaining of feeling unusually tired. Olive gave him some warm milk and put him to bed in the sunny front room of the house.

That evening Jemima and her family arrived, including John Jones, the doctor. John offered Daniel some medicine, but Daniel refused to take it.

"No," he said. "I am not sick. I am worn out."

When Nathan came to see him, Daniel insisted on discussing the arrangements for his funeral. He then asked to be "fixed up" before he died. Olive arranged for a family slave to shave him, Jemima cut his hair, and his granddaughter Delinda brushed his teeth.

"See," he boasted. "These teeth would serve another body an entire other lifetime."

"Why don't you use them a while longer yourself, Grandpa?" Delinda asked.

Daniel just repeated his earlier statement: "No, I am about worn out."

As the night went on, more and more of the Boone clan gathered around Daniel, though no one could believe that anyone as alert and active as Daniel Boone was actually dying. In the morning Daniel requested a bowl of warm milk and then asked for all of his relatives and slaves to come to his bedside so that he could say good-bye to them.

"I have no fear of death," he told them. "All my life I have tried to do right and have struggled to pay my debts. I have been charitable to the poor, and now I trust in the mercy of God to reunite me with those who have gone before."

Then Daniel had a private word with each person as they all filed past his bed. When the last person had been spoken to, Jemima and Nathan each held one of his hands. Daniel turned to one and then to the other and, smiling, said, "I am going. My time has come."

Within a minute Daniel Boone was dead. It was September 26, 1820, one month before his eighty-sixth birthday.

Two days later another grandson-in-law, a Baptist minister named James Craig, presided over Daniel's funeral service. Flanders and Jemima Callaway's new barn was the only building in the area large enough to accommodate all the mourners.

Daniel Boone, the man who had spent his life in search of wilderness adventures and wide open spaces, would be laid to rest beside his faithful wife and partner, Rebecca. When the funeral service was over, several hundred people walked a mile to the burial site. Even after his death, where Daniel Boone went, people followed.

Bibliography

Draper, Lyman C. *The Life of Daniel Boone.* Stackpole Books, 1998.

Faragher, John Mack. *Daniel Boone: The Life and Legend of an American Pioneer.* Henry Holt and Company, 1992.

Van Noppen, John James, and Ina Woestemeyer. *Daniel Boone: Backwoodsman.* The Appalachian Press, 1966.

Grateful acknowledgement is given to Daniel Boone historian Ken Kamper for supporting research in this revised edition. Kamper is director of the Daniel Boone and Frontier Families Research Association in Herrmann, Missouri.

About the Authors

Janet and Geoff Benge are a husband and wife writing team with more than thirty years of writing experience. Janet is a former elementary school teacher. Geoff holds a degree in history. Together they have a passion to make history come alive for a new generation of readers.

Originally from New Zealand, the Benges make their home in the Orlando, Florida, area.

Heroes of History are available in paperback, e-book, and audiobook formats, with more coming soon! Unit Study Curriculum Guides are available for each biography.

www.HeroesThenAndNow.com

Also from Janet and Geoff Benge...

More adventure-filled biographies for ages 10 to 100!

Gladys Aylward: The Adventure of a Lifetime • 978-1-57658-019-6
Nate Saint: On a Wing and a Prayer • 978-1-57658-017-2
Hudson Taylor: Deep in the Heart of China • 978-1-57658-016-5
Amy Carmichael: Rescuer of Precious Gems • 978-1-57658-018-9
Eric Liddell: Something Greater Than Gold • 978-1-57658-137-7
Corrie ten Boom: Keeper of the Angels' Den • 978-1-57658-136-0
William Carey: Obliged to Go • 978-1-57658-147-6
George Müller: Guardian of Bristol's Orphans • 978-1-57658-145-2
Jim Elliot: One Great Purpose • 978-1-57658-146-9
Mary Slessor: Forward into Calabar • 978-1-57658-148-3
David Livingstone: Africa's Trailblazer • 978-1-57658-153-7
Betty Greene: Wings to Serve • 978-1-57658-152-0
Adoniram Judson: Bound for Burma • 978-1-57658-161-2
Cameron Townsend: Good News in Every Language • 978-1-57658-164-3
Jonathan Goforth: An Open Door in China • 978-1-57658-174-2
Lottie Moon: Giving Her All for China • 978-1-57658-188-9
John Williams: Messenger of Peace • 978-1-57658-256-5
William Booth: Soup, Soap, and Salvation • 978-1-57658-258-9
Rowland Bingham: Into Africa's Interior • 978-1-57658-282-4
Ida Scudder: Healing Bodies, Touching Hearts • 978-1-57658-285-5
Wilfred Grenfell: Fisher of Men • 978-1-57658-292-3
Lillian Trasher: The Greatest Wonder in Egypt • 978-1-57658-305-0
Loren Cunningham: Into All the World • 978-1-57658-199-5
Florence Young: Mission Accomplished • 978-1-57658-313-5
Sundar Singh: Footprints Over the Mountains • 978-1-57658-318-0
C.T. Studd: No Retreat • 978-1-57658-288-6
Rachel Saint: A Star in the Jungle • 978-1-57658-337-1
Brother Andrew: God's Secret Agent • 978-1-57658-355-5
Clarence Jones: Mr. Radio • 978-1-57658-343-2
Count Zinzendorf: Firstfruit • 978-1-57658-262-6
John Wesley: The World His Parish • 978-1-57658-382-1
C. S. Lewis: Master Storyteller • 978-1-57658-385-2
David Bussau: Facing the World Head-on • 978-1-57658-415-6
Jacob DeShazer: Forgive Your Enemies • 978-1-57658-475-0

Isobel Kuhn: On the Roof of the World • 978-1-57658-497-2
Elisabeth Elliot: Joyful Surrender • 978-1-57658-513-9
D. L. Moody: Bringing Souls to Christ • 978-1-57658-552-8
Paul Brand: Helping Hands • 978-1-57658-536-8
Dietrich Bonhoeffer: In the Midst of Wickedness • 978-1-57658-713-3
Francis Asbury: Circuit Rider • 978-1-57658-737-9
Samuel Zwemer: The Burden of Arabia • 978-1-57658-738-6
Klaus-Dieter John: Hope in the Land of the Incas • 978-1-57658-826-2
Mildred Cable: Through the Jade Gate • 978-1-57658-886-4
John Flynn: Into the Never Never • 978-1-57658-898-7
Richard Wurmbrand: Love Your Enemies • 978-1-57658-987-8
Charles Mulli: We Are Family • 978-1-57658-894-9
John Newton: Change of Heart • 978-1-57658-909-0
Helen Roseveare: Mama Luka • 978-1-57658-910-6
Norman Grubb: Mission Builder • 978-1-57658-915-1
Albert Schweitzer: Le Grand Docteur • 978-1-57658-961-8
Frederick Douglass: The Right to dignity • 978-1-62486-151-2

Available in paperback, e-book, and audiobook formats.